THE ESSENTIAL

D0176535

West Highland White Terrier

The West Highland White Terrier's Senses

SIGHT

West Highland White Terriers can detect movement at a greater distance than we can, but they can't see as well up close. They can also see better in less light, but can't distinguish many colors.

SOUND

Westies, like all dogs, can hear about four times better than we can, and they can hear high-pitched sounds especially well.

TASTE

West Highland White Terriers have fewer taste buds than we do, so they're likelier to try anything—and usually do, which is why it's important for their owners to monitor their food intake. Dogs are omnivorous, which means they eat meat as well as vegetables.

TOUCH

Westies are social animals and love to be petted, groomed and played with.

SMELL

A West Highland White Terrier's nose is his greatest sensory organ. A dog's sense of smell is so great he can follow a trail that's weeks old, detect odors diluted to one-millionth the concentration we'd need to notice them, even sniff out a person under water!

Getting to Know Your West Highland White Terrier

Before you make arrangements to visit a breeder, now is the ideal time to learn as much about Westies as you can. The purpose of this chapter is to give you the answers you need so that you will not have a shred of doubt about whether the Westie is really the dog you want.

THE WORD THAT SAYS IT BEST

What is it really like to live with a Westie? If any experienced Westie owner had to come up with a one-word answer to that question, the word would have to be *fun*. Westies approach life and the world with a happy, lighthearted attitude that is downright contagious.

Remember that a Westie does not realize he weighs less than twenty pounds. As a result, a Westie often thinks of himself as equal to anything any dog is called upon to do. They are ideal pets for town, suburbs or country. Many Westies divide their time between city homes during the week and a getaway place in the country on weekends—and they adapt to both wonderfully well. To a Westie, the number one priority is to be close to the people he loves best, so if you like to jog or take hikes in the country, your Westie will want in on the fun and he *will* be able to keep up.

And that's regardless of the season. A Westie in the snow is a sight to behold—running, jumping and rolling about in the drifts. When he is done being the *abominable snow-dog,* he will be covered from head to toe with the cold, wet stuff and as happy as can be. When you see this, you won't be able to help smiling yourself and sharing your Westie's joy of living even though you are going to be the one to towel him dry!

In addition, Westies love a long walk or a safe run off-lead. Checking out all the delicious smells and chasing squirrels are all important Westie agenda items.

A DOG FOR THE WHOLE FAMILY

A Westie is a dog for the entire family. They can rough and tumble with the best of them and can be peaceful and quiet when called upon to be.

The Westie can stand up to the rowdy play of teenagers and usually understands how to behave around younger children. Many senior citizens own Westies and find them wonderful, understanding companions who bring a sunny outlook into

When there is a Westie in your home, life is bright for everyone the dog touches.

lives that so need it. Many Westies owners use their pets as Therapy Dogs, visiting local hospitals and nursing homes.

A TRUE TERRIER PERSONALITY

If you are considering a Westie pet, you must first like terriers or any dog with an active, get-up-and-go outlook on life. If your idea of a good pet is one who lies at your feet and is a passive presence in your life, you will have to take the time to train your Westie to lie down quietly and calmly. This is fairly easy to accomplish, but it will take a small time investment on your part.

Westies Do Bark

People often speak disparagingly of "yappy little terriers," but what these critics fail to realize is that there were good reasons for Westies and related breeds to be vocal when they routinely did a terrier's work. The nature of the breed goes back to working requirements.

Any dog going to ground was required either to kill the quarry underground or alert the huntsman to the location of the prey so that it

Teach your young child to handle your Westie puppy gently and lovingly and they will be best friends for life!

3

could be dug out and dispatched. Naturally, the dog would accomplish any required signaling by loud, persistent barking. To those hunters, the terrier with the big voice and the inclination to use it was considered valuable to any hunting effort.

Most Westies are never used for work, but they are still equipped for their traditional calling, and that includes the use of their voice. It is a fact: Westies are vocal, some more than others, but a Westie needs little encouragement to express his own opinion about the affairs of his world. Of course, this means that a Westie is usually a very keen watchdog. His size rules out

These Westies want to know who or what is lurking on the other side of this fence.

4

Exercise Requirements

Even though a Westie is small, he is active and loves being on the go. A Westie should have several good walks on-lead every day or access to a fenced yard or dog run.

A healthy adult Westie will do fine with three or four daily walks, at least one of which should be fairly long. Walking on a leash provides rhythmic exercise for your dog and is beneficial for you, too. Who knows, you may even get to meet other Westie enthusiasts on your way. It doesn't even have to be a nice day for a Westie to have a good exercise session. You may not appreciate a walk in snow or bracing cold, but Westies will like it just fine.

Your Westie will also love to have you throw a favorite toy for him to catch and bring back for another toss. It's great fun and a good way for your Westie to exercise, but you and your pet may come to a clash of wills on the matter of when the game should end.

Never, under any circumstances, should any Westie be allowed to run off-lead where he cannot be kept under control. This little dog is amazingly quick and can be off and away in the blink of an eye

his effectiveness as a guard dog (though not in his opinion), but that loud bark is often enough to discourage intruders.

The downside is that not everyone can be expected to understand or appreciate the reason for the breed's vocal nature. If you live in a high-rise apartment building and spend a good deal of your time out of your apartment, your Westie in these circumstances might bark from boredom or in response to every passing footstep. The result can be some unhappy neighbors, and a sticky situation for you. Luckily, it is a fairly easy prospect to train your Westie to "speak" and "shush" on command and thus teach him the right times to bark.

regardless of how well trained he is. The sight of a cat or another dog will trigger those dormant terrier instincts, and more than one free-running Westie has come to grief under the wheels of a passing car.

Westies Dig

We must also consider the terrier trait of digging. Digging is part of a terrier's job description. Westies, like most other terrier breeds, were meant to dig.

It is possible to curtail the digging to a certain extent, but it cannot be doused altogether. For Westies having access to a fenced yard, measures must be undertaken to dog-proof the yard to prevent digging escape tunnels. Of course, the considerate thing to do from your Westie's viewpoint is to provide a digging pit (much like a child's sand pit) and bury toys, treats and bones there. Your Westie will soon learn that his digging pit is a virtual treasure trove and almost all digging will be limited to the appropriate area.

WESTIES WITH OTHER PETS

Just as barking and digging are natural actions for terriers, hunting and

Westies, like all dogs, love to exercise and play.

CHARACTERISTICS OF A WESTIE

Energetic

Hearty

Fun-loving

Affectionate

Adaptable

Loves to dig and hunt

You can count on your Westie to bring love, cheer and friendship into your home when you most need it!

killing what they consider vermin are also second nature.

If you are adding a Westie puppy to your household and own a cat or two, it is sometimes best for the animals to arrange their own social hierarchy. If you are adding a kitten to a home with a Westie already in it, you should make introductions slowly and supervise them carefully.

If you are bringing a Westie into a home with small animal pets (for example, gerbils or hamsters), you should relocate these animals so that they are Westie-proof. A high shelf would do nicely.

WHAT YOUR WESTIE CAN MEAN TO YOU

The world according to the Westie is a world of activity and a celebration of life. This small, rough-coated being gives his people the outer limits of his adoration. You can spend a long, frustrating day dealing with the cares of the world, but come home to your Westie and you'll soon be reminded of how wonderful your pet knows you to be. Just turn the key in the lock and your Westie will issue a fanfare of joyous barks that chase away, if only briefly, the worries of a larger world.

Perhaps that's the reason that once a person allows a Westie into his or her life, often another will follow. Like the potato chip ad that challenges us to eat just one, Westies give so much pleasure that many people imagine that if one is great, two must be terrific. To the true Westie lover, no other breed fits the bill for a companion quite as well.

Homecoming

What an exciting time! You are about to bring your new Westie home. Considering the Westie's average longevity, you can expect at least thirteen years of love and companionship from this dog.

SETTING UP FOR YOUR PUPPY

Before you bring your new puppy home, decide which spot in your home will be her special place. Like all dogs, Westies are social beings, so it's best if they have human company as much as possible. The spot you choose should be public enough to give your puppy the feeling of being a full part of family life, but out of

the way enough so that she can rest as needed. The puppy's spot should be dry and draft-free, easily reached from any part of your home and easily cleaned.

You may want to look into a puppy playpen. This is an enclosure similar to a wire crate, but larger. It allows the puppy room to play, access to water, toys and food, and a "potty corner" if you want; it will

In a wild setting, canines make their home in a den; a crate offers the Westie the same feeling of security and protection.

keep puppy out of trouble with electric wires, chair legs and other favorite chewables. For Westies, even adults, two-by-three feet or three-by-three feet does nicely.

Getting It Straight About the Crate

It is good to see dog owners developing the right attitude about the place of a crate in the life of a pet dog. There was a time when many people were horrified at the suggestion that new puppy owners acquire crates for their pets. The thinking then was that this apparatus was a cage, representing cruelty and confinement. Actually, nothing could be further from the truth when a crate is used correctly. In a wild setting, canines make their home in a den.

The den is where they sleep, eat and bear and raise their young. It provides security and protection for them. In the same way, your puppy's crate is her safe haven in your home and beyond.

By feeding your puppy in her crate, you make the crate that much more attractive. Feeding the puppy in the crate also gives her a chance to have peaceful, uninterrupted meals.

A crate helps tremendously with housetraining. A healthy dog or puppy will usually not soil her sleeping place and when at home keep your puppy in her crate as much as possible. Not only will this help to avoid accidents and reprimands, and strengthen a growing puppy's physical control. But by taking her to her doggy toilet (at least once an hour) you get to show her where to go and to reward her for going in the right place. Offer your Westie three liver treats each time she does the right thing in the right place at the right time, and she will be housetrained in no time!

A crate is also the most effective protection for a dog in a vehicle. It acts as a seat belt for the dog, and also makes bringing the dog along safer and easier for the driver.

PUPPY ESSENTIALS

To prepare yourself and your family for your puppy's homecoming, and to be sure your pup has what she needs, you should obtain the following:

Food and Water Bowls: One for each. We recommend stainless steel or heavy crockery—something solid but easy to clean.

Bed and/or Crate Pad: Something soft, washable and big enough for your soon-to-be-adult dog.

Crate: Make housetraining easier and provide a safe, secure den for your dog with a crate—it only looks like a cage to you!

Toys: As much fun to buy as they are for your pup to play with. Don't overwhelm your puppy with too many toys, though, especially the first few days she's home. And be sure to include something hollow you can stuff with goodies, like a Kong.

I.D. Tag: Inscribed with your name and phone number.

Collar: An adjustable buckle collar is best. Remember, your pup's going to grow fast!

Leash: Style is nice, but durability and your comfort while holding it count, too. You can't go wrong with leather for most dogs.

Grooming Supplies: The proper brushes, special shampoo, toenail clippers, a toothbrush and doggy toothpaste.

9

PUPPY-PROOFING YOUR HOME

Provide a safe environment for your Westie. A good rule of thumb when you are preparing your home for a new puppy is to take the same precautions you would for an active toddler. Keep electrical cords taped up out of the puppy's reach. Make sure you stow all household cleaners, detergents, paints, lawn products, medicines and any other potentially dangerous chemicals securely away. Antifreeze, slug bait and rat poisons are especially dangerous. If you have a fenced yard, remember that

Westies are excellent diggers, so you might want to sink some wire around the perimeter of the yard to discourage an escape attempt. Failing that, you might consider fencing off a small part of your yard as an exercise area.

BRINGING YOUR WESTIE PUPPY HOME

When your new puppy first arrives home, give her the opportunity to rest, especially if your trip home has been a long one. The puppy will need to relieve herself and will

Stock up on safe chew toys for your Westie, so this doesn't happen to your sneakers!

definitely need some quiet time. Many well-meaning new owners, in the excitement of the moment, show the new puppy to all the neighbors and their children's friends. This is the wrong thing to do. A puppy is a baby and doesn't know what to make of this strange place and these strange people. It's much better to give the puppy the chance to rest up and then inspect a small portion of her new surroundings. It won't take long for the characteristic Westie self-confidence to kick in, but treating the puppy properly at the beginning is essential to get your relationship off on the right track.

The First Night

Some puppies will cry during the night for the first night or so, an understandable symptom of home-sickness and uncertainty. If your puppy does cry at night, don't go to her to comfort her. You will be let-ting the puppy know that it is okay to do this and encouraging the development of an undesirable habit. Do your best to ignore the crying if it happens. You may want to keep the puppy's crate in your bedroom for the sake of a night's

HOUSEHOLD DANGERS

Curious puppies and inquisitive dogs get into trouble not because they are bad, but simply because they want to investigate the world around them. It's our job to protect our dogs from harmful substances, like the following:

In the Garage

antifreeze

garden supplies, like snail and slug bait, pesticides, fertilizers, mouse and rat poisons

In the House

cleaners, especially pine oil

perfumes, colognes, aftershaves

medications, vitamins

office and craft supplies

electric cords

chicken or turkey bones

chocolate, onions

some house and garden plants, like ivy, oleander and poinsettia

11

sleep. If she starts to cry, just put your hand on the crate reassuringly, but don't take her out. Try to get something that has the smell of the puppy's first home on it and place this in the crate.

IDENTIFY YOUR DOG

It is a terrible thing to think about, but your dog could somehow, someday, get lost or stolen. For safety's sake, every dog should wear a buckle collar with an identification tag. A tag is the first thing a stranger will look for on a lost dog. Inscribe the tag with your dog's name and your name and phone number.

There are two ways to permanently identify your dog. The first is a tattoo, placed on the inside of your dog's thigh. The tattoo should be your Social Security number or your dog's AKC registration number. The second is a microchip, a rice-sized pellet that is inserted under the dog's skin at the base of the neck, between the shoulder blades. When a scanner is passed over the dog, it will beep, notifying the person that the dog has a chip. The scanner will then show a code, identifying the dog.

ESTABLISH A ROUTINE

If you always remember that dogs are creatures of habit, you will be able to establish a good routine that your Westie will be happy with and you can handle easily.

Rigid adherence to a schedule is not realistically possible, but the routine should be followed as closely as possible, especially in terms of housetraining. Take your puppy to the yard or walk her at the same times every day. Feed your Westie puppy at the same times every day and use the same food or combination of food.

Leaving Your Puppy Alone

Eventually, you will have to leave your puppy alone. To teach your puppy to enjoy time at home alone, practice short periods of confinement to her crate (plus a stuffed chew toy) when you are at home. When leaving, reassure the puppy that you will not be gone long, and leave a radio on during your absence. The music and human voices will help keep your puppy reassured while you are away from her. If you will be gone for only a short while—say, no more than an hour—you can safely confine the puppy to her crate. For longer absences, use a playpen or confine the puppy to a small area with an easily cleaned floor. If you decide to use a bathroom or laundry room, you are well-served to use an expandable baby gate across the

These little ones are adjusting well to their new home and family.

door and get items such as towels or scatter rugs out of harm's way. Keep the crate in the room with the puppy, with the door open. If you leave her stuffed chew toys, the puppy will have plenty to occupy herself with.

CONGRATULATIONS

You and your new Westie puppy are on the brink of a wonderful life adventure. Your puppy is ready to give her all for you, and you must be ready to do everything you can to ensure that she lives a long, happy life. If you have any questions at all, check with the breeder who sold you your puppy, your veterinarian or a dog trainer in your local area who has had experience with Westies.

You will soon learn how bright your new Westie friend really is and will come to appreciate the rich dimension she adds to your life. Take the good advice of your dog's

Training sessions are part of this Westie's daily routine.

breeder and your vet and your trainer, and have confidence in your ability to provide all that your Westie needs. You are about to have a wonderful experience that you will always remember.

To Good Health

Today, the owner of a West Highland White Terrier is truly fortunate, and for many reasons. Given a reasonable level of consistent, attentive care, most Westies will enjoy at least a dozen happy years.

Another reason for the good fortune of today's Westie owner is one shared by all dog owners. Modern advances in veterinary science have done for our dogs what advances in human medicine have done for us. Today, your Westie can look forward to a lifetime of better health care in both routine and unusual situations.

PREVENTIVE CARE

The easiest way to make sure your Westie remains healthy and sound is to make preventive care a priority from the start.

Choose a knowledgeable veterinarian, and establish a good working relationship with him or her. Follow the vaccination schedule you devise with your vet, and be sure to follow up with boosters when necessary. Examine your Westie from head to tail everyday (and check for cuts, lumps and parasites) when you groom him.

Keeping your puppy's environment safe and clean will do much to minimize potential hazards. Keep your puppy on a leash or in an enclosed yard, and make sure he has some basic obedience training

VACCINATIONS

One of the most important items on your agenda on the day you get your new Westie puppy is to get a copy of his health records. This will include the types and names of all inoculations, and when they were given, as well as a complete list of wormings. Take this to your veterinarian on your first visit, and she or he will set up a schedule to continue these inoculations.

The diseases your puppy needs to be vaccinated against include distemper, hepatitis, parainfluenza and leptospirosis. All the diseases your puppy needs protection from have specific symptoms and means of transmission. Remember all these diseases are extremely serious (most are fatal) and they are all easily preventable with vaccinations.

Locating the right veterinarian is a matter of the highest priority for you and your Westie.

Distemper is a viral disease and is highly contagious and is spread by canine urine and feces An affected dog will run a high fever, cough, vomit, have diarrhea and seizures. These symptoms will worsen, ultimately leading to death.

Hepatitis is a most serious liver disorder characterized by fever, abdominal pain, vomiting and diarrhea.

Parainfluenza, also known as "kennel cough," is not a particularly debilitating upper respiratory infection characterized by a dry, nonproductive cough, but it is extremely infectious. The mode of inoculation for parainfluenza is usually through the nostrils, with a specially adapted syringe tip. Because there are so many strains of this disease (much like the flu in humans), one vaccine cannot prevent them all. However, if you are planning on making any kind of trip to another location or will be boarding your puppy in a kennel facility, a parainfluenza shot is necessary.

Leptospirosis is a bacterial disease spread by the urine of infected animals. Mice and rats are especially implicated in transmission, so protection is a good idea. This is

ADVANTAGES OF SPAY/NEUTER

The greatest advantage of spaying (for females) or neutering (for males) your dog is that you are guaranteed that your dog will not produce puppies. There are too many puppies already available for too few homes. There are other advantages as well.

Advantages of Spaying

No messy heats.

No "suitors" howling at your windows or waiting in your yard.

No risk of pyometra (disease of the uterus) and decreased incidences of mammary cancer.

Advantages of Neutering

Decreased incidences of fighting, but does not affect the dog's personality.

Decreased roaming in search of bitches in season.

Decreased incidences of many urogenital diseases.

particularly important for Westies, since they will relentlessly seek out rats and mice and their environment. Pest control! It's a good idea to speak to the vet about this vaccination, since leptospirosis shots sometimes results in a bad reaction in the puppy.

Parvovirus and **coronavirus** have become noteworthy health problems among companion dogs. Both diseases are extremely infectious and spread by canine feces. Affected dogs show a high fever and bloody and/or mucoid diarrhea. Their behavior is lethargic, and they are in great peril as these dangerous diseases are often fatal. Happily, there is protection against both these killers.

Dog owners are required by law to have their pets inoculated for **rabies.** This disease is characterized by altered behavior; shy animals may appear friendly or aggressive. As the virus spreads, the animal will begin to salivate excessively and drool. The virus is spread through the animal's saliva. There is no cure for rabies in dogs. People who have been bitten by a rabid animal must endure a long and painful series of shots. This is one vaccine that is not optional, with good reason!

Booster Shots

After your puppy gets his first permanent shot, he should have an annual booster. Always keep your

Keep to your vaccination schedule religiously, and don't let your puppy outdoors until your veterinarian says you can.

Westie's shots current. You open a door to disaster for your pet when you let boosters slide.

INTERNAL PARASITES

There's no getting away from it— worms are a fact of life, but you can do a lot to make sure they don't cause problems for your Westie.

When you pick up your puppy, you should be given, along with the vaccination schedule, the dates of the puppy's previous wormings and the names of the drugs that were used. When you take your new puppy to the veterinarian for that first check-up, take his medical history, and take along a stool sample as well. The veterinarian will examine it and determine what kind of worms, if any, are present. She or he will also give you the appropriate medicine and instruct you on the dosage.

In most cases, worming a puppy is a pretty straightforward matter, and today's medications are much easier on a puppy's delicate system than were the remedies of years ago. Don't ignore a worm infestation, but know that such conditions are not unusual and will respond to proper treatment.

YOUR PUPPY'S VACCINES

Vaccines are given to prevent your dog from getting infectious diseases like canine distemper or rabies. Vaccines are the ultimate preventive medicine: They're given before your dog ever gets the disease so as to protect him from the disease. That's why it is necessary for your dog to be vaccinated routinely. Puppy vaccines start at 8 weeks of age for the five-in-one DHLPP vaccine and are given every three to four weeks until the puppy is 16 months old. Your veterinarian will put your puppy on a proper schedule and will remind you when to bring in your dog for shots.

Roundworms

These worms are extremely common and can infest even unborn puppies, passing through the placenta to establish themselves. In heavy infestations, it is not unusual to see live roundworms in a puppy stool. Roundworms can even be vomited up. They get their name by their tendency to curl up when exposed to air. Symptoms of roundworm infestation include a pot belly and a dull coat. Diarrhea and vomiting are other clues to the presence of these worms. For puppies, roundworms can be especially serious, so if your puppy has them, act fast.

19

Tapeworm

Tapeworm is another common internal parasite and is usually spread by fleas, which act as intermediate hosts. A dog troubled with a flea infestation may swallow some fleas while biting at itchy flea bites, and in the process ingest tapeworm eggs. Tapeworms are long, segmented parasites, and the fresh, moving segments are often plainly visible in a stool. Dried segments stuck to the dog's hair near the anus resemble grains of brown rice. A tapeworm-affected dog may have diarrhea, dry skin or appear underweight. He may bite at his hindquarters or "scoot" them along the ground. Follow the veterinarian's directions and remember to treat your dog and household surroundings for fleas.

Hookworm

Hookworm is a common cause of anemia and is particularly devastating to young puppies. The parasite gets a good foothold when hygienic conditions are not observed or when dogs are exposed to contaminated areas. A dog may swallow larvae, or the worm may penetrate the dog's skin. Eggs are identifiable through microscopic examination from a fresh stool sample. Your veterinarian can dispense drugs to combat hookworm, but it is also necessary to keep your surroundings clean and prevent the puppy from contact with feces and other animals.

Whipworm

Suspect whipworm if your dog is passing a watery or mucoid stool, shows weakness, weight loss, general symptoms of anemia or appears to be in overall poor condition. Whipworm is not visible to the naked eye, so determination of infestation is up to your veterinarian and his or her microscope. If your dog does have whipworm, you will probably have to have several stool checks done and institute a regimen of medication prescribed by your veterinarian.

Treating your dog for whipworm, by itself, is not enough.

Whipworms, like so many other internal parasites, thrive in and are contracted from contaminated soil and unsanitary conditions. Sanitation and strict monitoring are important to keeping your dog clear of whipworm and all the other insidious parasites that can infest your dog.

Heartworm

The condition is passed by the bite of a mosquito infected with the heartworm larvae. It may take some time for the symptoms to show, and by the time adult worms take up residence in your dog's heart, heroic measures may be needed to restore a dog's health.

It is far easier and wiser to use preventive measures to protect your Westie from heartworm infestation. Your veterinarian will draw a blood sample from your dog at the appropriate time and examine it under a microscope for heartworm microfilaria. In the probable event that your dog is negative for heartworm, your veterinarian will dispense the pills or syrup your dog needs to remain free of the parasite.

Suspect heartworm if your dog exhibits a chronic cough and a general weakness, with an unexplained loss of weight.

Protozoans

Not all internal parasites are worms. Tiny, single-celled organisms called protozoans can also wreak havoc in your Westie's internal mechanisms, but effective treatment is available. The most common disorders in dogs caused by protozoans are coccidiosis and giardiasis.

Coccidiosis is generally the result of poor hygienic conditions in the dog's surroundings. The symptoms of this inflammation of the intestinal tract include sometimes bloody diarrhea, a generally poor appearance, cough, runny eyes and nasal and eye discharges. The disease is more serious in puppies, who are less resistant.

Giardiasis comes from drinking water contaminated with the disease-causing organism (usually from a stream). Giardia is nicknamed "beaver fever" because the organism is spread by beavers that relieve themselves in lakes and streams. As with coccidiosis, diarrhea—the color of milk chocolate—is a symptom. A vet must make the definite diagnosis.

21

EXTERNAL PARASITES

Fleas

For your Westie, a good scratch is one of life's little pleasures. However, if your Westie appears to be spending a lot of time scratching himself and doing so with a vengeance, you should take a closer look. If your Westie's skin looks red and irritated and there are little dark flecks throughout his coat, fleas may have set up housekeeping with your pet as their primary host. Bad news? Absolutely, but there are things you can do about it.

First, treat your dog. He should be dipped and given a good bath with a flea and tick shampoo. Be cautious here as some preparations will turn a Westie's coat pink. Luckily, nowadays there are several easy-to-administer systematic treatments (available from your vet), which make your dog flea-free.

Getting the fleas off your Westie alone is not enough. You must also treat your home and yard. Destroy any contaminated bedding, and go over the dog's entire environment with a spray or fogger to kill all the fleas. This means outdoors as well as inside the home.

Ticks

Ticks look like tiny spiders. They attach themselves to a passing dog, suck blood from the dog, mate, and drop off, and the females lay thousands of eggs to begin the life cycle yet again. In the course of feeding, the female, which is much larger than the male, becomes engorged with blood. As with fleas, you must rid your dog and your environment of ticks if your control is to be effective.

Ticks are not as active as fleas, so removing them is a little easier.

This conscientious owner gives her Westie's coat and skin a routine once-over for skin disease and parasites.

Gently, but thoroughly comb your dog each time you return home from a walk during tick season. Go over the entire dog with a pair of tweezers; do not attempt to remove ticks with your fingers. Westie owners unlucky enough to have to deal with ticks can take comfort from the fact that the white coat makes it easier to find the little vampires. When you find a tick, drip a little alcohol directly on it. The alcohol will asphyxiate the tick, causing it to release its hold. Pull it off with tweezers, and drop the tick into a small cup of alcohol, where it will drown and trouble your dog no more.

Also remember that there are several kinds of ticks, and you should know which species are common to your area. The brown dog tick is probably the most common species, but there is a species that can spread Rocky Mountain Spotted Fever, and the tiny deer tick is the mode of transmission for Lyme disease. Lyme disease, like Spotted Fever, can be passed to humans, so be very careful if you find that your dog has a tick infestation. If your dog appears lame for no known reason, he may have contracted Lyme disease and will require veterinary attention.

FLEAS AND TICKS

There are so many safe, effective products available now to combat fleas and ticks that—thankfully—they are less of a problem. Prevention is key, however. Ask your veterinarian about starting your puppy on a flea/tick repellant right away. With this, regular grooming and environmental controls, your dog and your home should stay pest-free. Without this attention, you risk infesting your dog and your home, and you're in for an ugly and costly battle to clear up the problem.

In checking your Westie for ticks, pay particular attention to the face, the base of the ears, between the toes and the skin around the rear end—all places ticks seem to congregate.

Lice

Happily, these annoyingly persistent creatures are infrequently encountered in this age of enlightened hygiene. However, any dog can contract lice from any infested animal. Lice cause pronounced itching and are an annoying problem neither your dog nor you need. If your dog is harboring lice, treatment is the same as for fleas—a

23

good bath and a dip that does the job.

Mites

Mites infest different areas of a dog's body. You might say the various species are specialists of a sort.

The **ear mite** *(Otodectes cynotis)* is a common problem for dogs with dropped ears, but even Westies with their erect ears can be troubled by them. If your Westie seems constantly to be scratching at his ears and if, on examination, you notice a dark, crumbly, malodorous accumulation, your dog has ear mites and must be treated for them. Your veterinarian can give you medication and instructions for clearing up the problem.

Scabies, or sarcoptic mange, is yet another condition related to mite infestation. The causative agent, *Sarcoptes scabei,* is a microscopic organism that burrows under the host's skin, causing intense itching and hair loss. This condition can also be passed to humans. Left untreated, it can spread to a dog's entire body.

Demodetic mange is the name of the condition spread by *Demodex canis.* The mite lives in the dog's

hair follicles, causing hair loss and red, thickened skin. Eventually pustules form in infected follicles. Diagnosis via skin scrapings is required, and medicated dips are the treatment of choice to destroy these mites.

FIRST AID AND EMERGENCY CARE

Life for our dogs, as for us, always involves uncertainty. That is why you need to have some ability to minister to your dog in the event of a sudden illness or injury.

Muzzling

The first thing you should know how to do is to handle and transport an injured animal safely. A dog in pain is probably not going to recognize his owner or realize that people are trying to help him. In those circumstances, he is likely to bite. The dog in trouble needs to be muzzled.

Transporting Your Dog in an Emergency

An emergency stretcher can be made from a blanket and, depending on the size of the dog, carried by

24

two or more people. An injured dog can also be carried on a rigid board, in a box or wrapped in a towel and carried in a person's arms. Care should be taken, though, that the manner of transport does not exacerbate the dog's original injury.

Shock

If a dog is in shock, keep him as warm and as quiet as possible and get him emergency veterinary attention at once.

Bleeding

If your dog is bleeding, direct pressure is an effective way to staunch the flow. You can fashion a pressure dressing from gauze or some strong fabric. Wrap the area of the wound, applying even pressure as you apply the gauze strips. If you notice tissue swelling below the site of the wound, ease the pressure or, if necessary, remove the bandage altogether. If you have no gauze, use any clean cloth or your hand as a last resort. For arterial bleeding, you will probably need a tourniquet along with the pressure bandage. You may use gauze strips, cloth or

WHEN TO CALL THE VETERINARIAN

In any emergency situation, you should call your veterinarian immediately. Try to stay calm when you call, and give the vet or the assistant as much information as possible before you leave for the clinic. That way, the staff will be able to take immediate, specific action when you arrive. Emergencies include:

- Bleeding or deep wounds
- Hyperthermia (overheating)
- Shock
- Dehydration
- Abdominal Pain
- Burns
- Fits
- Unconsciousness
- Broken bones
- Paralysis

any other material that can be wrapped tightly between the wound and the heart to slow the flow of blood. With a tourniquet, you must remember to loosen the pressure about every ten minutes. Get the injured dog to a veterinarian as soon as possible.

WHAT'S WRONG WITH MY DOG?

We've listed some common conditions of health problems and their possible causes. If any of the following conditions appear serious or persist for more than 24 hours, make an appointment to see your veterinarian immediately.

CONDITIONS	POSSIBLE CAUSES
DIARRHEA	Intestinal upset, typically caused by eating something bad or overeating. Can also be a viral infection, a bad case of nerves or anxiety or a parasite infection. If you see blood in the feces, get to the vet right away.
VOMITING/RETCHING	Dogs regurgitate fairly regularly (bitches for their young), whenever something upsets their stomach, or even out of excitement or anxiety. Often dogs eat grass, which, because it's indigestible in its pure form, irritates their stomachs and causes them to vomit. Getting a good look at *what* your dog vomited can better indicate what's causing it.
COUGHING	Obstruction in the throat; virus (kennel cough); roundworm infestation; congestive heart failure.
RUNNY NOSE	Because dogs don't catch colds like people, a runny nose is a sign of congestion or irritation.
LOSS OF APPETITE	Because most dogs are hearty and regular eaters, a loss of appetite can be your first and most accurate sign of a serious problem.
LOSS OF ENERGY (LETHARGY)	Any number of things could be slowing down your dog, from an infection to internal tumors to overexercise—even overeating.

Diarrhea

Diarrhea is often the normal result of your dog having eaten something he shouldn't have. However, it can also be the symptom of something more serious, and in young puppies, it can cause dehydration quickly. If

CONDITIONS	POSSIBLE CAUSES
STINKY BREATH	Imagine if you never brushed your teeth! Foul-smelling breath indicates plaque and tartar buildup that could possibly have caused infection. Start brushing your dog's teeth.
LIMPING	This could be caused by something as simple as a hurt or bruised pad, to something as complicated as hip dysplasia, torn ligaments or broken bones.
CONSTANT ITCHING	Probably due to fleas, mites or an allergic reaction to food or environment (your vet will need to help you determine what your dog's allergic to).
RED, INFLAMED, ITCHY SPOTS	Often referred to as "hot spots," these are particularly common on coated breeds. They're caused by a bacterial infection that gets aggravated as the dog licks and bites at the spot.
BALD SPOTS	These are the result of excessive itching or biting at the skin so that the hair follicles are damaged; excessively dry skin; mange; calluses; and even infections. You need to determine what the underlying cause is.
STINKY EARS/HEAD SHAKING	Take a look under your dog's ear flap. Do you see brown, waxy buildup? Clean the ears with something soft and a special cleaner, and don't use cotton swabs or go too deep into the ear canal.
UNUSUAL LUMPS	Could be fatty tissue, could be something serious (infection, trauma, tumor). Don't wait to find out.

diarrhea continues for more than twenty-four hours, or if you notice any other symptoms, call your vet immediately.

Broken Bones

With fractures, you must determine how to help the dog without doing more harm than good. The area of the fracture should be immobilized with the use of a splint or a rolled-up magazine secured with gauze or similar material, and the area should be cushioned to support it as much as possible. In compound fractures, the broken bone will pierce the skin; this is more serious than a simple fracture and should be covered in preparation for transfer to a veterinarian. Fractures are very painful, and the injured dog must be handled with great care and probably muzzled for the safety of all who will handle him.

Heatstroke

The Westie's system is admirably suited to the cold, but far less efficient in heat. Dogs can die from heatstroke easily. Regardless of the season, a dog showing signs of heat distress—rapid, shallow breathing and a rapid heartbeat—needs to be cooled down immediately. Spraying or soaking the dog with cold water, or pressing an ice bag or freezer pack against the groin, abdomen, anus, neck and forehead are all effective in bringing down the stricken dog's temperature.

Choking

If your Westie is choking, you must act quickly to find and dislodge the foreign object after securing the mouth open by inserting a rigid object between the molars on one side. Use your fingers or, very carefully, use long-nosed pliers or a hemostat to withdraw the object. The Heimlich maneuver can also be used for choking dogs; ask your veterinarian to demonstrate how it's done.

Convulsions

Dogs going through convulsions should be cushioned to avoid self-injury, and you must avoid putting a hand near the mouth of a seizuring

Keep your Westie's double coat cool while he plays outdoors.

28

dog. Such dogs are not likely to swallow their tongues during an episode, but it is a wise idea to have the dog examined by a veterinarian to determine the cause and means of control. Canine convulsions often respond to a drug-based therapy. See your veterinarian as soon as possible to evaluate the problem and begin a course of appropriate medication.

Lameness

A Westie can go lame for a wide variety of reasons. He can cut a pad, pick up a foreign body (like a thorn) or break a nail. All these things will cause lameness. For cuts, clean the area and apply an antiseptic. If the wound is deep, staunch the bleeding and get your Westie to the vet. Also, for a painful broken nail, visit your veterinarian as soon as possible. He or she will medicate the injury to promote healing. With a broken nail, the vet will trim off as much as possible and cauterize and wrap the dog's paw.

Insect Bites

If your Westie is bitten by any sting-ing insect, remove the stinger, apply a baking soda paste to the affected

POISON ALERT

If your dog has ingested a potentially poisonous substance, waste no time. Call the National Animal Poison Control Center hot line:

(800) 548-2423 ($30 per case) or

(900) 680-0000 ($20 first five minutes; $2.95 each additional minute)

area and stop the swelling and pain with an ice bag or cold pack. It would be a wise idea to run your pet's wounds past your vet to be sure all is well. An antibiotic may be prescribed.

Bee stings are painful, but even more serious is the possibility that your dog is allergic to them. If so, the sting will start to swell immedi-ately. If this happens, get your Westie to the vet as soon as possible. He or she will administer an anti-histamine or other treatment.

Vomiting

Your dog will regurgitate when he eats something he shouldn't have, and this is usually nothing to worry about. However, if the vomitus looks bloody or otherwise unusual, call your vet immediately. If your dog

29

PREVENTIVE CARE PAYS

Using common sense, paying attention to your dog and working with your veterinarian, you can minimize health risks and problems. Use vet-recommended flea, tick and heartworm preventive medications; feed a nutritious diet appropriate for your dog's size, age and activity level; give your dog sufficient exercise and regular grooming; train and socialize your dog; keep current on your dog's shots; and enjoy all the years you have with your friend.

has been throwing up, you may want to help him along to recovery by feeding a bland diet of moist rice with a little chicken. You may want to add a tablespoon of yogurt to help restore helpful microbes to the digestive tract. If your dog vomits more than once, take him to the vet.

HEREDITARY PROBLEMS OF THE WEST HIGHLAND WHITE TERRIER

The West Highland White Terrier does present a number of health concerns, but in general this is a trouble-free breed and most Westies live to a ripe old age.

Skin Diseases

Skin disease does occur in this breed. The Westie is a white, harsh-coated dog, and both these characteristics are conducive to skin troubles. The exact problem may not manifest itself until long after you have acquired your Westie. A skin disease is usually controllable by diet, medication, medicated baths or a combination of these. If your Westie is suffering from a skin disorder, you must find out exactly what problem you are dealing with. Take your dog to a veterinary dermatologist.

Help is available. The West Highland White Terrier Club of America maintains a special task force called W.A.T.C.H., which is concerned with this and other aspects of Westie wellness. Call W.A.T.C.H. at 1-800-4-WESTIE.

Cranio Mandibular Osteopathy (CMO)

The bad news about CMO is that it is a painful inflammation of the lower jaw, causing difficulty in chewing and swallowing. The good news about the disease is that it is almost always seen in growing puppies and disappears by the time the dog is 8 or 9 months old. Treatment is with drugs dispensed by your veterinarian.

CMO, also known as "lion jaw," is not seen until the puppy is several months old and probably in a new home. Even if your Westie's parents have a history of CMO, there is no way of knowing whether it will appear in their offspring or in which ones. If your Westie gets it, you should definitely tell the breeder about the situation.

Legg-Perthes' Disease

Legg-Perthes' disease is the necrotic degeneration of the femoral head. In plain English, that means that the head of the femur (the part of the upper hind-leg bone that fits into the pelvis) crumbles from a cutoff in the blood supply. This may be genetically transmitted, or it may be as a result of trauma. There is no documented proof to certify or disprove either claim. Possibly, Legg-Perthes' can come from either cause. In any case, an affected dog will begin to limp and develop progressively less use of the affected leg. Treatment is via surgical removal of the damaged head and a conservative

exercise regimen. Recovery is usually complete and rapid.

Legg-Perthes' disease is another condition that does not manifest itself until the puppy is more than 6 or 7 months old, by which time most pet Westies will be in their new homes. The puppy's breeder may have had experience with Legg-Perthes', or this may be the first case. Regardless, let the breeder know about it.

Luxating Patella

The patella is the kneecap and, in ordinary circumstances, it slides up and down in front of the knee joint.

Learning how to properly care for your Westie's health will enable him to enjoy a long, full, happy life with his family.

With a number of small breeds, including Westies, it will slide from its normal position toward the inner leg. The most obvious symptom is the onset of limping. A dog may or may not exhibit pain during these episodes. Luxating patella is a recurring condition that could eventually lead to arthritis; the only permanent cure is surgical correction of the affected knee. Sensible weight control and reasonable exercise levels will also benefit the affected individual.

Dry Eye

Science calls this disorder *keratitis sicca,* but whatever one calls it, it means the lack of production of

This woman carefully applies eye drops to her Westie's eye.

tears. Obviously, this condition is very uncomfortable, and left untreated could cause permanent damage to the eye itself. Treatment consists of lubricating the eye with a number of daily applications of a special solution of "artificial tears" to keep the eye moist. One can also have surgery performed that involves resectioning the salivary glands.

CARE OF THE SENIOR CITIZEN

The Westie senior citizen will spend more time sleeping. He may not be as attentive to your comings and goings as he did when he was younger. He may walk more slowly with a few more halting steps than the hellion of a puppy you remember from a decade ago.

Make sure his bed is comfortable and located in a draft-free spot. Also remember that a Westie is never too old to be a busybody, so keep his bed where he can keep up with family activity. A small artificial lambskin rug would be especially appreciated on cold nights.

Now is a good time to talk to your veterinarian about your aging Westie's diet. Tell the vet what you are feeding when you bring him in for a checkup, and ask his or her advice about changing food.

Carefully monitor your Westie and groom him frequently. Watch his teeth and keep them clean. If any appear broken or rotten, have them extracted. Your Westie will be happier and healthier as a result.

Make it a point to check your Westie's vision and hearing regularly. Cataracts are a common consequence of aging in dogs. Your Westie may lose all or part of his vision, but if you have him in familiar surroundings, he will probably get along just fine.

This senior Westie still has what it takes to be a loyal and playful companion!

33

EUTHANASIA

Sometimes a well-loved old dog peacefully slips away in his sleep. Often though, an old dog is brought to the veterinarian's office for euthanasia. Euthanasia (painless death) is a prospect every dog owner must face sooner or later.

The time to consider euthanasia for your dog is when his quality of life is no longer sufficient. Many owners are guilty of thinking more of their own feelings than their dogs' when they elect to delay the inevitable. Remember, your Westie

has a sense of only the present and the past. He lives today and does not have a handle on the future. For him, the end of life holds no terrors. Euthanasia is not painful, but an old dog's confusion can be terribly stressful. When the sedative is administered, show your dog the loyalty he has shown to you. Stay with him. Let yours be the last voice he hears. You'll be doing the right thing, and you owe it to your dog.

ANOTHER WESTIE

If yours was a one-Westie household, you will probably want another to fill the empty space left by your

This little guy is up to the challenge of squirming his way into someone's heart.

old friend. The time to seek a new Westie is for you to determine, but it is better to let a little time go by. This way, you give yourself a chance to heal from the loss of your old pet and allow the newcomer to make his own inroads on your heart in his own ways and for his own reasons.

Positively Nutritious

The importance of good feeding is obvious, but the rules for maintaining a dog on good food and a sensible feeding regimen are wonderfully simple. It is when dog owners start making up their own rules about feeding that good husbandry can become derailed.

Over the course of a dog's life, her nutritional requirements will change just as ours do, and it is important to be aware of those needs ahead of time. If you approach the entire matter of feeding from a commonsense point of view and arm yourself with good information, you can expect that your dog will be properly fed for her entire life.

GROWTH STAGE FOODS

Once upon a time, there was puppy food and there was adult dog food. Now there are foods for puppies, young adults/active dogs, less active dogs and senior citizens. What's the difference between these foods? They vary by the amounts of nutrients they provide for the dog's growth stage/activity level.

Less active dogs don't need as much protein or fat as growing, active dogs; senior dogs don't need some of the nutrients vital to puppies. By feeding a high-quality food that's appropriate for your dog's age and activity level, you're benefiting your dog and yourself. Feed too much protein to a couch potato and she'll have energy to spare, which means a few more trips around the block will be needed to burn it off. Feed an adult diet to a puppy, and risk growth and development abnormalities that could affect her for a lifetime.

What and how much you feed your Westie largely depends on her stage of development.

FEEDING YOUR WESTIE PUPPY

If you are about to get your first West Highland, you will surely want to know just what to do to make sure you feed her properly. Before you bring her home, ask what she is being fed and when, and stick to the same food and routine after you get her home. Do this for at least the first week or so.

In most cases, the puppy you get will be on three meals a day. Stick to this number of feedings as much as possible. A Westie puppy will continue to grow until she is about 9 months old, and it is important to feed with this fact in mind. You may need to change feeding times to accommodate your own lifestyle. No problem. Just make sure that you ease the puppy into your requirements. Making abrupt changes can be stressful and physically upsetting for the puppy.

The three-meals-a-day routine should be followed until the puppy reaches about 6 months of age. At this point, put her on a morning and an evening meal until she reaches her first birthday. At a year of age, she will do well on one meal a day,

Put your Westie's nutritional needs first on your priority list.

with biscuits in the morning and at bedtime. However, if you prefer to keep your Westie on two meals a day, there is no reason not to.

WHAT TO FEED YOUR WESTIE

Today, we and our dogs benefit from extensive research that has been conducted to find the best foods available for routine, day-to-day feeding, as well as foods for growing puppies, geriatrics, dogs with specific health needs and dogs with high levels of activity. The various dog food companies have gone to con-siderable expense to develop nutritionally complete, correctly balanced diets for all dogs.

Dry Food (Kibble)

The basis of your dog's diet should be dry kibble. A high-quality, well-balanced kibble is nutritionally complete and will be relished by your dog under all normal conditions. Most major dog food companies manufacture a special formulation to meet the explosive growth of young puppies. These are highly recommended for daily feeding up to your Westie's first birthday. Use

HOW TO READ THE DOG FOOD LABEL

With so many choices on the market, how can you be sure you are feeding the right food to your dog? The information is all there on the label—if you know what you're looking for.

Look for the nutritional claim right up top. Is the food "100 percent nutritionally complete"? If so, it's for nearly all life stages; "growth and maintenance," on the other hand, is for early development; puppy foods are marked as such, as are foods for senior dogs.

Ingredients are listed in descending order by weight. The first three or four ingredients will tell you the bulk of what the food contains. Look for the highest-quality ingredients, like meats and grains, to be among them.

The Guaranteed Analysis tells you what levels of protein, fat, fiber and moisture are in the food, in that order. While these numbers are meaningful, they won't tell you much about the quality of the food. Nutritional value is in the dry matter, not the moisture content.

In many ways, seeing is believing. If your dog has bright eyes, a shiny coat, a good appetite and a good energy level, chances are her diet's fine. Your dog's breeder and your veterinarian are good sources of advice if you're still confused.

the puppy foods. They work! For a mature dog, choose a kibble with a minimum of 20 percent protein. This and other important nutritional information will be on the label.

Many experienced dog keepers are firm believers in feeding dry kibble, or just flavoring it slightly with broth or canned meat to heighten palatability. Others, just as adamantly, insist that the dog is a natural meat eater and her diet should contain significant amounts of fresh or canned meat. Actually, a diet that mixes both meat and kibble is likely to provide your dog with the best features of both foods. If one had to come down on the side of one food or the other, the winner would have to be an all-kibble diet. Studies have shown that dogs raised on all-meat diets often suffer from malnutrition and serious deficiencies, which may cause extreme physically debilitating problems.

Adding Canned Food or Meat

If you decide to add meat to the food, the best choice is beef. It may be freshly cooked, if you like, or canned. There are some very fine canned meats available, and it is a good idea for you to check the label, looking for about 10 percent protein. Chicken is also a good food source and is available in canned form. If you cook any poultry for your Westie, bone it carefully. The same is true for fish, which most dogs relish. Cottage cheese is another good protein source, especially for puppies or dogs convalescing from illness.

Water

Besides feeding a high-quality food, you must keep ample clean, fresh water available for your dog at all times. It is vital to do so.

ESTABLISHING A FEEDING SCHEDULE

Establishing a feeding schedule depends on the demands of your own daily routine. Whatever time you decide, feed at the same time every day. Dogs are creatures of habit and are happiest when maintained on a specific schedule. Of course, there will be days when you can't be there to feed your pet at her regular dinner hour. It's okay. An

39

This Westie puppy can count on having her meals at the same time every day and has access to fresh, cool water at all times.

TYPES OF FOODS/TREATS

There are three types of commercially available dog food—dry, canned and semimoist—and a huge assortment of treats (lucky dogs!) to feed your dog. Which should you choose?

Dry and canned foods contain similar ingredients. The primary difference between them is their moisture content. The moisture is not just water. It's blood and broth, too, the very things that dogs adore. So while canned food is more palatable, dry food is more economical, convenient and effective in controlling tartar buildup. Most owners feed a 25 percent canned/75 percent dry diet to give their dogs the benefit of both. Just be sure your dog is getting the nutrition she needs (you and your veterinarian can determine this).

Semimoist foods have the flavor dogs love and the convenience owners want. However, they tend to contain excessive amounts of artificial colors and preservatives.

Dog treats come in every size, shape and flavor imaginable, from organic cookies shaped like postmen to beefy chew sticks. Dogs seem to love them all, so enjoy the variety. Just be sure not to overindulge your dog. Factor treats into her regular meal sizes.

occasional break in the routine is not a disaster, as long as your dog knows that most of the time she will be fed at a set time.

HOW MUCH TO FEED YOUR WESTIE

The amount of food you feed your Westie depends on the individual dog: her age, health, stage of life and activity level.

If your Westie is very active, she will burn more calories and need more food than a house pet who doesn't get extraordinary amounts of exercise. There will be a difference in the eating patterns of a growing puppy and an elderly animal. If your dog is ill or convalescing, her food needs will also differ from the requirements of a healthy animal. Use your own educated judgment.

If a healthy dog cleans her bowl but still appears hungry, she might need a little more to reach the right amount of daily ration. Adjust accordingly.

Another way to determine whether you are feeding the right amount of food is to let the dog's condition tell you. If your dog is healthy but appears thin, you may want to feed a bit more. If the dog looks to be on the plump side, a more restricted diet is in order. If you can't feel your dog's ribs beneath her fur, she's overweight. Weigh your dog, get your vet's advice and start her on a diet right away.

PEOPLE FOOD

It can be okay to offer human food at times and to add table scraps occasionally to your dog's food, but do it wisely and in moderation. Dogs like carrots, broccoli and other fresh vegetables; some even like fruits. These are okay, as are bits of cooked meat (no bones). And remember all those balanced rations mentioned earlier in this chapter: Quality food made specifically for dog feeding will do a better job of nourishing your pet than treats you may feel good about offering.

BONES

On the matter of bones, your Westie is infinitely better off without them. Certain beef bones are safe enough, but others, such as poultry, chop or fish bones, are definitely dangerous and should never be offered. If you need another reason to keep bones away from your Westie, think of what a greasy mess a Westie who has been playing with a big soup bone can become. If you can't visualize it,

FOOD ALLERGIES

If your puppy or dog seems to itch all the time for no apparent reason, she could be allergic to one or more ingredients in her food. This is not uncommon, and it's why many foods contain lamb and rice instead of beef, wheat or soy. Have your dog tested by your veterinarian, and be patient while you strive to identify and eliminate the allergens from your dog's food (or environment).

trust me—it's not pretty, and there are many safe chewing items you can give your Westie that she will enjoy every bit as much. Alternatively, bury the bones in your Westie's digging pit—what a delightful surprise!

This nutrition-savvy owner feeds her Westie from a measuring cup to keep track of how much her pet eats.

41

Putting on the Dog

If you are considering owning a Westie based on pictures you've seen or dogs you've observed, you

should remember that Westies don't just grow that way. Proper care involves regular grooming, and regular grooming involves a certain level of commitment. A well-groomed Westie is one of the most delightful-looking of all dogs.

THE WESTIE'S COAT

A Westie normally carries two coats—a thick, soft undercoat closer to the skin, and a harsh, longer coat that is what we see. In the Scottish Highlands, the undercoat kept the dog warm and dry while the outercoat protected him from thorns, brambles, dirt and sometimes even the teeth of other animals. The climate where you live may be very different from that of the Westie's native home, but the coat is still the same. The undercoat remains fairly constant at all times, but the over-coat grows until the hairs reach a certain length. At that point, the coat is blown (falls out) or dies and must be removed to make room for a fresh, new "jacket."

DO-IT-YOURSELF GROOMING, YES OR NO?

You'll perform routine grooming at home, but you need to decide in advance who will provide the more intensive grooming your dog must have.

If you are good with your hands, you might enjoy trying your hand at trimming. You will enjoy a greater closeness with your Westie and save money at the same time. If you would rather leave the trimming to someone else, find a qualified groomer nearby.

When selecting a groomer, be sure the person knows specifically how to groom a Westie. Many a Westie pet owner has gone to the grooming shop to collect their pride and joy, only to be greeted by a pet

The more a Westie is groomed, the better he will look, and the healthier his skin and coat will be.

43

who now resembles a caricature of a Scottie or a Schnauzer. The profes-sional who grooms your dog should know how to make a Westie look the part.

ROUTINE GROOMING

Routine grooming should be done at home. It's easy, it's relaxing and it promotes the health and cleanliness of your Westie and the closeness of your relationship.

Ideally, daily grooming is won-derful, but not really necessary. If you can thoroughly groom your pet two or three times a week, he will

GROOMING TOOLS

pin brush	scissors
slicker brush	nail clippers
flea comb	tooth-cleaning equipment
towel	shampoo
mat rake	conditioner
grooming glove	clippers

This Westie stands on a grooming table for a safe and more comfortable session.

44

get on just fine and you will be rewarded by the pride you take in him.

Grooming for a Westie consists, mainly, of brushing and combing.

The rest involves trimming, nail and foot care and cleaning of ears and teeth. Bathe your Westie only when and if it is necessary. Often, Westies can be made to look sparkling without ever getting near the bathtub. Keep reading and you'll know how.

Grooming Supplies

There are several tools you will need to make the most of your Westie's appearance. As you develop confidence and proficiency, you may add your own touches to your tool kit and your grooming skills. For starters, though, you'll need the following:

- A good-quality chrome-plated steel comb
- A soft-bristle slicker brush
- A pin brush or wig brush
- A pair of small barber's shears
- A pair of single serrated thinning shears
- A nail clipper for dogs
- Cotton
- Corn starch or powdered chalk or talc
- No-rinse dog shampoo

The pin brush is used mostly on the head, legs and skirt (hair under the tummy).

45

Grooming the Westie Puppy

Always groom your puppy on a sturdy table with a nonskid surface. He will be safer if you do and offer less resistance to what is basically an unfamiliar ritual.

Never walk away from a dog on the grooming table. He may jump off and injure himself seriously. In a restraint, he may try to jump and accidentally hang himself if you are not close by.

When you start the grooming, talk kindly to your puppy, pick up your soft slicker brush and go over

This owner uses a slicker brush and encouraging words to acclimate her Westie puppy to grooming.

QUICK AND PAINLESS NAIL CLIPPING

This is possible if you make a habit out of handling your dog's feet and giving your dog treats when you do. When it's time to clip nails, go through the same routine, but take your clippers and snip off just the ends of the nail—clip too far down and you'll cut into the "quick," the nerve center, hurting your dog and causing the nail to bleed. Clip two nails a session while you're getting your dog used to the procedure, and you'll soon be doing all four feet quickly and easily.

46

The guillotine clipper, like the one shown here, is the most popular clipper used by dog owners.

the entire body coat, brushing from head to tail. On the legs and head, brush against the lie of the coat. Now, with the metal comb, gently comb down the leg furnishings and, if there is enough hair, fluff up the hair on the head. If not, go through the motions to acclimate the puppy to what is to come.

Always keep these sessions brief, lengthening them as the puppy grows and develops more patience and confidence. The main purpose is to teach the youngster to accept grooming and keep him clean. Never do anything to a young puppy on the table that will make him resent or fear grooming sessions.

When you are done, take him off the table and tell him how handsome he is and how pleased you are with him. You might even want to reward him with a small treat. In this way, your Westie will always be a pleasure to groom and a source of pride to his entire family.

Grooming the Adult Westie

After your Westie has matured to the point at which he has enough hair for you to really get working on, start by misting the entire coat with water. You don't need to drench him; the point is to be able to brush him thoroughly without breaking the hairs or damaging the coat. After misting him, do a quick once-over with a natural bristle brush to help get the water through the coat.

Follow this with another once-over, this time with a pin brush. After using the pin brush, use your slicker over the entire dog—grooming with the lie of the coat on the body and the skirt, and against the grain on the head and legs.

Follow this up with a light combing mainly to smooth down the leg furnishing and skirt and make them blend in with the body coat. Do this two or three times a week (more often, if you like) and your Westie will never develop unsightly, uncomfortable mats, and you will also be on top of any skin problems or unwelcome invasions by external parasites.

GROOMING FOR GOOD HEALTH

Eyes

Generally speaking, there is little the owner needs to do to care for a Westie's eyes. It is normal for a small amount of matter to collect at the inner corner of the eyes. Check this every ten days or so, and gently remove any accumulation with a moistened cotton ball. If there appears to be considerable amounts of matter, or if the matter is wet and mucousy, you might want to call it to the attention of your veterinarian. If there is a problem, he or she can prescribe an appropriate medication and regimen.

Ears

During a thorough grooming session, check your Westie's ears. Healthy ears are clean, free of debris and without odor. If necessary, gently pluck out any long hair that you can grasp growing from the ear canal. Wipe out the canal with a cotton ball moistened with a little alcohol. If you keep to this regimen, your Westie should never be troubled with ear infections. If you notice your Westie shaking his head or pawing at his ears, or if you notice a dark discharge at the ear opening or an unpleasant odor, a trip to the veterinarian is in order.

47

KEEPING YOUR WESTIE WHITE

Bathing Your Westie

For most pet owners, keeping a dog clean means bathing, but bathing your Westie too often is not a great idea. When a bath is needed there is a right way to do it. Here's how.

After a thorough brushing, put the dog in the sink or tub and insert cotton in his ears to keep the water out.

Now you are ready to bathe him, but don't fill the sink at all. Most kitchen sinks have a spray hose, or you can buy one. Adjust the water to be a little hotter than lukewarm, and wet the dog's body thoroughly with the hose, saving the head for last. After the coat is thoroughly wet, pour a small amount of shampoo made for white dogs down the spine and, using a sponge, lather thoroughly, working with the lie of the coat. Make sure you soap the skirt and the legs. Save the head for last, taking care to keep water out of the ears and the eyes.

Now rinse out all the shampoo. If the dog still looks a bit dingy, repeat the process. After you have rinsed all the shampoo out of the coat, squeeze as much excess moisture from the skirt and legs as you can, wrap the dog in a large towel and blot the towel over him to keep from getting soaked yourself.

Use a hose to wet down your Westie.

Pour a small amount of shampoo made for white dogs and work up to a lather.

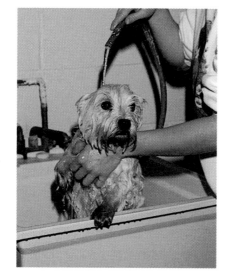

CLOSING THOUGHTS ON GROOMING A WESTIE

You are probably reading this book because you are considering getting a pet you want to be proud of, or because you already have a Westie and are proud of him. Think how your pride will be enhanced when you know your saucy, white-coated friend is aware of his good looks and overall well-being. A few short sessions every week to groom your Westie will make him look his best. Then, as you stroll through the park or the mall together, you can enjoy the admiring glances your

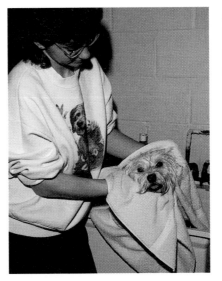

Rinse your Westie thoroughly and gently towel-dry him.

49

handsome, well-cared-for Westie is bound to attract. It's a lovely experience; promise yourself you'll try it soon.

You look marvelous!

Measuring Up

The West Highland White Terrier is one of a group of small, active dogs originally developed to pursue and eliminate small animals that could make life uncomfortable around the homes and farmsteads of Scottish country folk. The breed's purpose in life made it essential for her to be sturdy and courageous, and to be equal to both a harsh environment and the fierce adversaries she was meant to exterminate.

To fully understand and appreciate just what a Westie is, it is necessary to understand something of the breed's original function and how her conformation and temperament relate to what she was bred to do.

THE STANDARD FOR THE WESTIE

When the West Highland White became known to the world beyond heather and mist, her supporters wrote a word picture of the ideal specimen and used it as a guide for breeders and judges. Ultimately, this word picture evolved into what fanciers call the standard of the breed. Every American Kennel Club (AKC) recognized breed has a standard. This standard describes in detail not only the breed's physical features but its temperament as well.

The standard for the West Highland White Terrier, in one version or another, has been used around the world for close to a century to define and describe the breed for all who love and care about the Westie. In the following discussion of the standard, the official standard appears in italics and the author's comments follow in regular type. For a copy of the complete standard, contact the West Highland White Terrier Club of America (see chapter 9, "Resources," for the address).

THE AMERICAN KENNEL CLUB

Familiarly referred to as "the AKC," the American Kennel Club is a nonprofit organization devoted to the advancement of purebred dogs. The AKC maintains a registry of recognized breeds and adopts and enforces rules for dog events including shows, obedience trials, field trials, hunting tests, lure coursing, herding, earthdog trials, agility and the Canine Good Citizen program. It is a club of clubs, established in 1884 and composed, today, of over 500 autonomous dog clubs throughout the United States. Each club is represented by a delegate; the delegates make up the legislative body of the AKC, voting on rules and electing directors. The American Kennel Club maintains the Stud Book, the record of every dog ever registered with the AKC, and publishes a variety of materials on purebred dogs, including a monthly magazine, books and numerous educational pamphlets. For more information, contact the AKC at the address listed in Chapter 9, "Resources."

General Appearance

The West Highland White Terrier is a small, game, well-balanced, hardy looking terrier, exhibiting good showmanship, possessed with no small amount of self-esteem.

This section describes an attractive, no-nonsense working terrier. She must be of a size to "go to ground"—that is, small enough to fit into the dens and burrows of the animals she was meant to pursue.

She must also be "game"—brimming with courage and confidence, essential in a dog who was meant to tackle tough, determined prey.

Along with small size and gameness, the Westie should give the

WHAT IS A BREED STANDARD?

A breed standard—a detailed description of an individual breed—is meant to portray the ideal specimen of that breed. This includes ideal structure, temperament, gait, type—all aspects of the dog. Because the standard describes an ideal specimen, it isn't based on any particular dog. It is a concept against which judges compare actual dogs and breeders strive to produce dogs. At a dog show, the dog that wins is the one that comes closest, in the judge's opinion, to the standard for its breed. Breed standards are written by the breed parent clubs, the national organizations formed to oversee the well-being of the breed. They are voted on and approved by the members of the parent clubs.

Today's Westie is usually not called upon to work, but she should have the build and the heart to fill the breed's time-honored function.

appearance of hardiness. She's a tough nut. Cold doesn't stop her, wet doesn't stop her and obstacles don't stop her. She exhibits in marked degree a combination of strength and activity.

Size, Proportion and Substance

The ideal size is between eleven inches at the withers for dogs and ten for bitches. The Westie is a compact dog, with good balance and substance. Short-coupled and well boned.

The Westie is a small dog who should be substantial enough to perform the breed's work with relative ease. The breed standard is silent on the matter of weight, but specifies an ideal height of 11 inches for males (dogs) and 10 inches for females (bitches), with a slight deviation being acceptable. The height is measured at the top of the shoulders (withers). A Westie should be short-coupled, which means that the body should be compact, with no obvious length. The Westie should also have sturdy bones so that you immediately get an impression of exceptional strength for a dog of this size.

Head

*Shaped to present a round appearance from the front. Should be in proportion to the body. **Expression**—Piercing, inquisitive, pert.*

Although the standard calls for a rounded appearance, this is achieved more through trimming than conformation. The head should also be in pleasing proportion to the body, neither too small nor "pinheaded," nor too large and overdone. The expression is a combination of self-confidence and impish good humor.

EYES

Widely set apart, medium in size, almond shaped, dark brown in color, deep set, sharp and intelligent.

There should be considerable space between the eyes on a good Westie head. Viewed head-on, the outer corner of the eyes should align approximately with the inner corner of the ears. The eyes are medium sized, almond shaped and dark brown. Sharp and intelligent, they look out from under heavy brows, producing a piercing look. The eye rims are black. Small, full or light-colored eyes are considered faulty according to the breed standard.

The first thing most people will notice on a Westie is the roundness of the head.

53

EARS

Small, carried tightly erectly, set wide apart, on the top outer edge of the skull. They terminate in a sharp point and must never be cropped.

The Westie's ears should be small, held tightly erect and set wide apart on the top outer edge of the skull. If this is hard for you to visualize, think of the ears being placed at the corners of the head.

The ears should end in a sharp point, although some groomers prefer to take a tiny bit of hair from the very tip to make for a slightly rounded, more natural effect. Westie ears are always naturally erect and are never cropped. They are

This pup's ears are beginning to come up and will soon be carried sharply erect as required by the standard.

powerful and taper gradually to the large, black nose. The jaws are level and powerful. Lips are black.

Bite—The teeth are large for the size of the dog. A tight scissors bite with upper incisors slightly overlapping the lower incisors or level mouth is equally acceptable.

Bite is important to any terrier. In Westies, the teeth are surprisingly big, considering the small size of the dog. The bite should be either scissors (upper incisors slightly overlapping lowers) or level (incisors meeting tip to tip). Both types are equally acceptable.

Body

Neck—Muscular and well set on sloping shoulders. Topline—Flat and level, both standing and moving. Body—Compact and of good substance.

A Westie should have a muscular neck smoothly set on sloping shoulders. The neck is neither too short nor too long and should be in good proportion to the entire dog. The topline, which is the area of the back from behind the shoulders to the base of the tail, is flat and level, standing and moving.

It is important for the Westie to have a compact, substantial body.

trimmed short, with the hair smooth and velvety, free of fringe at the tips.

SKULL

Broad, slightly longer than the muzzle, not flat on top but slightly domed between the ears. Muzzle—Blunt, slightly shorter than the skull, powerful and gradually tapering to the nose.

A Westie's skull tapers gradually to the eyes. There is a definite indentation, called a stop, where the skull and the muzzle join. The skull is finished off with heavy eyebrows. A long or narrow skull is considered a fault.

The muzzle is blunt and slightly shorter than the skull. It should be

The ribs are deep and well-arched in their upper half (extending at least to the elbow). The dog's sides should appear flattish or somewhat heart-shaped. The back ribs are of considerable depth, and the distance from the last rib to the upper thigh is as short as possible while still allowing free movement. The chest is very deep, and the loin is short, broad and strong.

Tail

Relatively short, with good substance, and shaped like a carrot.

When the tail is held erect, it should never extend above the top of the skull. It is covered with short, hard hair with no fringe. The tail should be as straight as possible, carried gaily, but not curled over the back. Just as the Westie's ears are natural, the tail is never docked.

Forequarters

Shoulders—*Shoulder blades are well laid back and well knit at the backbone.* **Legs**—*Forelegs are muscular and well boned, relatively short but with sufficient length to set the dog up so as not to be too close to the ground.* **Feet**—*Forefeet are larger than the hind ones,*

are round, proportionate in size, strong, thickly padded.

A Westie's shoulders should be well-laid back, meaning that the tops point more to the base of the neck than further up the neck. The shoulders are well-knit at the backbone, meaning that the blades are close together at this point.

The Westie should have muscular forelegs with strong bones. The legs are relatively short, but long enough to set the dog up off the ground. The legs are reasonably straight and thickly covered with short, hard hair.

Feet are of great importance to a digging dog—they are the tools of her trade. A Westie's forefeet are noticeable larger than her hind feet, and are strong and tough looking. They may be turned out slightly. Dewclaws (the fifth digit) may be removed. Black pigmentation is most desirable on the pads of feet and nails, though black nails may fade as the dog ages.

Hindquarters

Thighs are very muscular, well angulated, not set wide apart. **Legs**—*Rear legs are muscular and relatively short and sinewy.*

Angulation refers to the degree of slope of a joint. The standard tells us a Westie's hindquarters should be "well-angulated." The Westie's hock (which corresponds to our heel) should extend beyond the buttocks and be parallel to the ground when the dog stands naturally.

Dewclaws may be removed from the back feet as with the front feet, but it is very rare to encounter them.

Coat

Very important and seldom seen to perfection. Must be double-coated. The head is shaped by plucking the hair, to present the round appearance. The ideal coat is straight, hard and white, but a hard coat which may have some wheaten is preferable to a white fluffy or soft coat.

The Westie's beautiful coat is a two-ply, or double, coat with a harsh outer layer and a softer undercoat. Both coats have a very specific purpose for the working terrier. The undercoat helps keep a dog warm and dry, while the outercoat protects the dog from brambles, rocky outcrops and, often, the teeth and claws of her prey.

As the breed name indicates, the color is ideally pure white, but many dogs with very hard outercoats will show some wheaten (straw-colored) tipping.

Today, Westies trimmed for the show ring are very tailored and stylized. While some purists bemoan this development, there is no need for the pet dog to be so treated. Your Westie will be just fine if her body coat is trimmed to neatness, her legs, feet and ears are neatly tidied and enough hair is left on the skull and around the head to act as a frame for the typical Westie expression.

Gait

Free, straight and easy all around. It is a distinctive gait, not stilted, but powerful with reach and drive.

Westies were meant to get along with each other and the people in their world.

The reason the Westie's coat is so important is because a good coat will keep a working terrier both warm and dry in the field. This well-turned-out pair both show the correct double coat.

Bear the Westie's work in mind once more and visualize a physically sound animal than can get from point A to point B with no physical strain whatever. A Westie's movement, like every other component of the breed, should call attention to her physical ruggedness and happy outlook on life.

Temperament

Alert, gay, courageous and self-reliant, but friendly. **Faults**—*Excess timidity or excess pugnacity.*

Consider the fact that in Scotland, Westies were traditionally worked in packs. To have a dog without courage or one more focused on fighting with the dog alongside her than at getting the game would have been counterproductive and would not have been tolerated. What the early breeders did for you and me by creating a dog with balanced characteristics was to give us an animal with unlimited terrier sparkle but not so fiery an attitude that owning the dog is a daily ordeal.

You will truly love your pet Westie for her wonderful personality. As you look for a puppy, keep that point foremost in your mind.

A Matter of Fact

When considering the history of the West Highland White, it is important to remember that we are dealing in possibilities, probabilities and a few Celtic legends thrown in. In all likelihood, the breed's earliest ancestor was a kind of generic Scotch Terrier. This ancestor probably most closely resembled the modern Cairn Terrier, but not that closely. Until the West Highland emerged as a distinct breed in the late nineteenth century, his ancestry is really a matter of conjecture.

THE FIRST SCOTTISH TERRIERS

Several centuries ago in Scotland and its Western Isles, terrier-type dogs were bred specifically to hunt and exterminate vermin. To the owners of these dogs, form and style were of little importance unless they contributed specifically to the dogs' function. Size was variable, and coat color and markings were varied and random. Those dogs bore little resemblance to the cultivated terriers familiar to us today.

Over a long period of time, terriers began to branch into distinctly different breeds. Terrier owners bred for certain characteristics over others, and the breeds began to differentiate. But it was still quite a melting pot. A dog's ancestry was whatever the owner, farmer or gamekeeper said it was.

We do know from historical records that terriers from Scotland were known from the days of Queen Elizabeth I and King James I. The court physician for Queen Elizabeth, Johannes Cauius (John Keyes), wrote the first dog book ever

This resting Westie is unaware of his hardworking terrier ancestors.

to be translated into English, *Of Englishe Dogges.* The book mentions "terrars from the barbarous borders northward," or terriers from Scotland. King James made a gift of white terriers from Argyllshire, Scotland, to the king of France. Correspondence regarding the King's generosity indicates that the gift was greatly appreciated.

THE EMERGENCE OF THE WESTIE

While the working terriers of Scotland were known in all colors and combinations of colors, in some places white was considered a mark of impurity. It was the practice of some breeders to destroy white puppies at birth.

One legend describes how this distasteful practice came to a well-deserved end. After returning from service in the Crimean War, Col. E. D. Malcolm, a venerable soldier and sportsman, was out hunting fox on his estate Poltalloch in Argyllshire. In the excitement of the hunt, Col. Malcolm shot at what he thought was a fox. It was one of the Colonel's favorite Cairns. With the tragic accidental death of this dog, the Colonel vowed from that

day forward to breed only the "whiteuns." This is generally credited with being the genesis of the West Highland White Terrier.

As the separate breeds emerged, they began to look less and less alike. The Scottish Terrier became heavier, lower to the ground and more substantial, with larger bones. The Cairn was smaller and longer in body. He remained most faithful to the old identity.

At the beginning of the twentieth century, some of the larger dog shows in England began to include classes for Westies, originally called Poltalloch Terriers. At the Crufts show in London in 1907, West Highlands received their own classification under the name West Highland White Terrier for the first time.

But even as the Westie emerged as a distinct breed, there are documented records of breedings involving Westies and Cairn Terriers and, in some instances, even Scotties. This situation existed until 1917, when the American Kennel Club stepped in and took the position that any English Westie showing one or more Cairn ancestors in its pedigree in the first three generations was ineligible for registration in this country. Before long, the Kennel Club in England could only go along with American policy and do likewise. The two breeds have been distinct ever since.

THE WESTIE IN AMERICA

The Westie's first appearance in the show ring occurred in England, but Americans were quick to recognize the breed's numerous virtues. The breed was shown at Westminster in 1906 under the name Roseneath Terrier, and was first listed in the AKC studbook two years later under the same name. The breed name was ultimately changed to West Highland White Terrier on May 31, 1909, and has remained so ever since. The West Highland White Terrier Club of America came into being in September 1909 and continues as the primary protector of the breed's fortunes in this country.

From the time the Westie was first recognized by the AKC, and up to the year 1962, the breed maintained moderate numbers and a small loyal following of enthusiasts. Under ordinary circumstances, that would not get a breed noticed when competing for attention with

WHERE DID DOGS COME FROM?

It can be argued that dogs were right there at man's side from the beginning of time. As soon as human beings began to document their existence, the dog was among their drawings and inscriptions. Dogs were not just friends, they served a purpose: There were dogs to hunt birds, pull sleds, herd sheep, burrow after rats—even sit in laps! What your dog was originally bred to do influences the way he behaves. The American Kennel Club recognizes over 140 breeds, and there are hundreds more distinct breeds around the world. To make sense of the breeds, they are grouped according to their size or function. The AKC has seven groups:

1. Sporting
2. Working
3. Herding
4. Hounds
5. Terriers
6. Toys
7. Non Sporting

Can you name a breed from each group? Here's some help: (1) Golden Retriever, (2) Doberman Pinscher, (3) Collie, (4) Beagle, (5) Scottish Terrier, (6) Maltese, and (7) Dalmatian. All modern domestic dogs (*Canis familiaris*) are related, however different they look, and are all descended from *Canis lupus*, the gray wolf.

Cockers, Boxers and other popular, established breeds of earlier decades.

61

Is it the Westie's adorable face or delectable personality that makes this breed one of today's most popular? You decide!

But the Westie had a friend in the James Buchanan Distilling Company of Glasgow, Scotland. Buchanan was the distiller of Black & White Scotch Whisky and used a Scottish Terrier and a West Highland White in an international advertising campaign that got the Westie noticed. *Life* magazine regularly featured ads showing the playful pair in all kinds of mischief, to sell the popular brand of scotch.

Famous artists of the day were commissioned to execute imaginative renderings. Morgan Dennis, a famous American illustrator, was closely associated with the black and white dogs, and his original works are highly prized by today's collector. Even copies of the magazine ads are in brisk demand, with many being framed, matted and hung in the homes of fanciers.

Because of the Black & White initiative, Westie lovers have, over the years, owned and enjoyed a variety of appropriately decorated barware that has been manufactured to promote the whisky. Many are avid collectors with amazing "toys" to show off.

WESTIE POPULARITY GROWS

Over the years, Westies made small, steady increases in popularity, but all that changed when a certain English Westie came to these shores in the late 1950s. His name was Elfinbrook Simon. Simon showed himself to be a first-class show dog and established himself as an important winner in a show career that is most conservative by today's standards. The high point of his career came in 1962 when Simon was Best-in-Show at the Westminster Kennel Club show, hosted by Madison Square Garden in New York City.

Simon was an electrifying showman and won the Garden in front of a TV audience of millions. After he was motioned to the winner's spot, he lifted his leg on the Best-in-Show sign and this brought the house down. No one ever forgot Westies after that "well-aimed" commentary.

In 1962, registrations jumped from 699 to 930. It was the biggest jump ever, and the Westie has never looked back. Now, more than thirty years later, the West Highland ranks in the upper one-fourth of all breeds registered with the AKC and is second among terrier breeds only to the Miniature Schnauzer.

Westies in Obedience

Westies are quite good in obedience, and many have won a number of

demanding titles in competition with all breeds. Whether you compete or not, remember to make training fun and interesting. Westies have nimble minds and need to be stimulated. A little legwork will help you find a local training class right in your community or not far away.

If, in the course of your training, you find that you and your dog like the work and function well as a team, you might want to look into obedience competition. The chances are excellent that the instructor can help you get started.

Make preliminary inquiries through your instructor or with the help of the West Highland White Terrier Club of America, whose name and address appear in chapter 9. The Club is very supportive of

This owner uses a food lure to train her puppy to sit.

A Westie demonstrates his agility ability.

tunnels, poles—and they dearly love the excitement of this popular, fast-growing sport. If agility sounds like something you and your Westie would enjoy doing, talk to others who are involved. Your advisers need not be Westie people, but a number of Westie enthusiasts have tried agility and find it right up the breed's alley.

Earthdog Trials

Very recently, the AKC has introduced a program into its series of performance events called earthdog trials. Obviously, this program is for small terriers and Dachshunds and is tailor-made for Westies. In earthdog trials, competitors are sent down a wooden tunnel at the end of which is a cage of rats. The object is to have the dogs go willingly into the tunnel, proceed quickly to the end and "give tongue" (bark) at the rats for a specified interval. There are a number of levels and titles available for competitors.

obedience and sponsors a large trial every October in conjunction with the club's national specialty show.

Agility

In canine agility, dogs must negotiate a series of obstacles—jumps,

CHAPTER EIGHT

On Good Behavior

by Ian Dunbar, Ph.D., MRCVS

Training is the jewel in the crown—the most important aspect of doggy husbandry. There is no more important variable influencing dog behavior and temperament than the dog's education: A well-trained, well-behaved and good-natured puppydog is always a

OWNING A PARTY ANIMAL

It's a fact: The more of the world your puppy is exposed to, the more comfortable she'll be in it. Once your puppy's had her shots, start taking her everywhere with you. Encourage friendly interaction with strangers, expose her to different environments (towns, fields, beaches) and most important, enroll her in a puppy class where she'll get to play with other puppies. These simple, fun, shared activities will develop your pup into a confident socialite; reliable around other people and dogs.

joy to live with, but an untrained and uncivilized dog can be a perpetual nightmare. Moreover, deny the dog an education and she will not have the opportunity to fulfill her own canine potential; neither will she have the ability to communicate effectively with her human companions.

Luckily, modern psychological training methods are easy, efficient, effective and, above all, considerably dog-friendly and user-friendly. Doggy education is as simple as it is enjoyable. But before you can have a good time play-training with your new dog, you have to learn what to do and how to do it. There is no bigger variable influencing the success

of dog training than the owner's experience and expertise. Before you embark on the dog's education, you must first educate yourself.

BASIC TRAINING FOR OWNERS

Ideally, basic owner training should begin well before you select your dog. Find out all you can about your chosen breed first, then master rudimentary training and handling skills. If you already have your puppydog, owner training is a dire emergency—the clock is ticking! Especially for puppies, the first few weeks at home are the most important and influential days in the dog's life. Indeed, the cause of most adolescent and adult problems may be traced back to the initial days the pup explores her new home. This is the time to establish the *status quo*— to teach the puppydog how you would like her to behave and so prevent otherwise quite predictable problems.

In addition to consulting breeders and breed books such as this one (which understandably have a positive breed bias), seek out as many pet owners with your breed as you can find. Good points are obvious.

66

What you want to find out are the breed-specific problems, so you can nip them in the bud. In particular, you should talk to owners with adolescent dogs and make a list of all anticipated problems. Most important, test drive at least half a dozen adolescent and adult dogs of your breed yourself. An 8-week-old puppy is deceptively easy to handle, but she will acquire adult size, speed and strength in just four months, so you should learn now what to prepare for.

Puppy and pet dog training classes offer a convenient venue to locate pet owners and observe dogs in action. For a list of suitable trainers in your area, contact the Association of Pet Dog Trainers (see chapter 9). You may also begin your basic owner training by observing other owners in class. Watch as many classes and test drive as many dogs as possible. Select an upbeat, dog-friendly, people-friendly, fun-and-games, puppydog pet training class to learn the ropes. Also, watch training videos and read training books. You must find out what to do and how to do it *before* you have to do it.

Socializing your Westie with as many people as you can will help develop her confidence and make her a more outgoing pet.

PRINCIPLES OF TRAINING

Most people think training comprises teaching the dog to do things such as sit, speak and roll over, but even a 4-week-old pup knows how to do these things already. Instead, the first step in training involves teaching the dog human words for each dog behavior and activity and for each aspect of the dog's environment. That way you, the owner, can more easily participate in the dog's domestic education by directing her to perform specific actions appropriately, that is, at the right time, in the right place and so on. Training opens communication channels, enabling an educated dog to at least understand her owner's requests.

In addition to teaching a dog what we want her to do, it is also necessary to teach her why she should do what we ask. Indeed, 95 percent of training revolves around motivating the dog to want to do what we want. Dogs often understand what their owners want; they just don't see the point of doing it—especially when the owner's

A well-trained, well-behaved and good-natured puppy-dog is always a joy to live with.

repetitively boring and seemingly senseless instructions are totally at odds with much more pressing and exciting doggy distractions. It is not so much the dog that is being stubborn or dominant; rather, it is the owner who has failed to acknowledge the dog's needs and feelings and to approach training from the dog's point of view.

The Meaning of Instructions

The secret to successful training is learning how to use training lures to predict or prompt specific behaviors—to coax the dog to do what you want when you want. Any highly valued object (such as a treat or toy) may be used as a lure, which the dog will follow with her eyes and nose. Moving the lure in specific ways entices the dog to move her nose, head and entire body in specific ways. In fact, by learning the art of manipulating various lures, it is possible to teach the dog to assume virtually any body position and perform any action. Once you have control over the expression of the dog's behaviors and can elicit any body position or behavior at will, you can easily

FINDING A TRAINER

Have fun with your dog, take a training class! But don't just sign on any dotted line, find a trainer whose approach and style you like and whose students (and their dogs) are really learning. Ask to visit a class to observe a trainer in action. For the names of trainers near you, ask your veterinarian, your pet supply store, your dog-owning neighbors or call (800) PET-DOGS (the Association of Pet Dog Trainers.)

teach the dog to perform on request.

Tell your dog what you want her to do, use a lure to entice her to respond correctly, then profusely praise and maybe reward her once she performs the desired action. For example, verbally request "Fido, sit!" while you move a squeaky toy upwards and backwards over the dog's muzzle (lure-movement and hand signal), smile knowingly as she looks up (to follow the lure) and sits down (as a result of canine anatomical engineering), then praise her to distraction ("Gooood Fido!"). Squeak the toy, offer a training treat and give your dog and yourself a pat on the back.

Being able to elicit desired responses over and over enables the owner to reward the dog over and over. Consequently, the dog begins to think training is fun. For example, the more the dog is rewarded for sitting, the more she enjoys sitting. Eventually the dog comes to realize that, whereas most sitting is appreciated, sitting immediately upon request usually prompts especially enthusiastic praise and a slew of high-level rewards. The dog begins to sit on cue much of the time, showing that she is starting to grasp the meaning of the owner's verbal request and hand signal.

You can get your dog to learn virtually any command by using a food lure. Look at this Westie go after his treat!

Why Comply?

Most dogs enjoy initial lure-reward training and are only too happy to comply with their owners' wishes. Unfortunately, repetitive drilling without appreciative feedback tends to diminish the dog's enthusiasm until she eventually fails to see the point of complying anymore. Moreover, as the dog approaches adolescence she becomes more easily distracted as she develops other interests. Lengthy sessions with repetitive exercises tend to bore and demotivate both parties. If it's not fun, the owner doesn't do it and neither does the dog.

Integrate training into your dog's life: The greater number of training sessions each day and the shorter they are, the more willingly compliant your dog will become. Make sure to have a short (just a few seconds) training interlude before every enjoyable canine activity. For example, ask your dog to sit to greet people, to sit before you throw her Frisbee and to sit for her supper. Really, sitting is no different from a canine "Please." Also, include numerous short training interludes during every enjoyable canine pastime, for example, when playing with the dog or when she is running in the park. In this fashion, doggy distractions may be effectively converted into rewards for training. Just as all games have rules, fun becomes training . . . and training becomes fun.

Eventually, rewards actually become unnecessary to continue motivating your dog. If trained with consideration and kindness, performing the desired behaviors will become self-rewarding and, in a sense, your dog will motivate herself. Just as it is not necessary to reward a human companion during an enjoyable walk in the park, or following a game of tennis, it is hardly necessary to reward our best friend—the dog—for walking by our side or while playing fetch. Human company during enjoyable activities is reward enough for most dogs.

Even though your dog has become self-motivating, it's still good to praise and pet her a lot and offer rewards once in a while, especially for a good job well done. And if for no other reason, praising and rewarding others is good for the human heart.

TRAINER'S TOOLS

Many training books extol the virtues of a vast array of training

This owner knows that the most effective way to instill good behavior in her Westie is to praise, praise, praise!

paraphernalia and electronic and metallic gizmos, most of which are designed for canine restraint, correction and punishment, rather than for actual facilitation of doggy education. In reality, most effective training tools are not found in stores; they come from within ourselves. In addition to a willing dog, all you really need is a functional human brain, gentle hands, a loving heart and a good attitude.

In terms of equipment, all dogs do require a quality buckle collar to sport dog tags and to attach the leash (for safety and to comply with

71

local leash laws). Hollow chew toys (like Kongs or sterilized longbones) and a dog bed or collapsible crate are musts for housetraining. Three additional tools are required:

1. specific lures (training treats and toys) to predict and prompt specific desired behaviors;

2. rewards (praise, affection, training treats and toys) to reinforce for the dog what a lot of fun it all is; and

3. knowledge—how to convert the dog's favorite activities and games (potential distractions to training) into "life-rewards," which may be employed to facilitate training.

The most powerful of these is knowledge. Education is the key! Watch training classes, participate in training classes, watch videos, read books, enjoy play-training with your dog and then your dog will say "Please," and your dog will say "Thank you!"

HOUSETRAINING

If dogs were left to their own devices, certainly they would chew, dig and bark for entertainment and

then no doubt highlight a few areas of their living space with sprinkles of urine, in much the same way we decorate by hanging pictures. Consequently, when we ask a dog to live with us, we must teach her *where* she may dig, *where* she may perform her toilet duties, *what* she may chew and *when* she may bark. After all, when left at home alone for many hours, we cannot expect the dog to amuse herself by completing crosswords or watching the soaps on TV!

Also, it would be decidedly unfair to keep the house rules a secret from the dog, and then get angry and punish the poor critter for inevitably transgressing rules she did not even know existed. Remember: Without adequate education and guidance, the dog will be forced to establish her own rules—doggy rules—and most probably will be at odds with the owner's view of domestic living.

Since most problems develop during the first few days the dog is at home, prospective dog owners must be certain they are quite clear about the principles of housetraining *before* they get a dog. Early misbehaviors quickly become established as the *status quo*—becoming firmly entrenched as hard-to-break bad habits, which set the precedent for years to come. Make sure to teach your dog good habits right from the start. Good habits are just as hard to break as bad ones!

Ideally, when a new dog comes home, try to arrange for someone to be present as much as possible during the first few days (for adult dogs) or weeks for puppies. With only a little forethought, it is surprisingly easy to find a puppy sitter, such as a retired person, who would be willing to eat from your refrigerator and watch your television while keeping an eye on the newcomer to encourage the dog to play with chew toys and to ensure she goes outside on a regular basis.

Potty Training

To teach the dog where to relieve herself:

1. never let her make a single mistake;

2. let her know where you want her to go; and

3. handsomely reward her for doing so: "GOOOOOOOD DOG!!!" liver treat, liver treat, liver treat!

HOUSETRAINING 1-2-3

1. Prevent Mistakes. When you can't supervise your puppy, confine her in a single room or in her crate (but don't leave her for too long!). Puppy-proof the area by laying down newspapers so that if she does make a mistake, it won't matter.

2. Teach Where. Take your puppy to the spot you want her to use every hour.

3. When she goes, praise her profusely and give her three favorite treats.

Preventing Mistakes

A single mistake is a training disaster, since it heralds many more in future weeks. And each time the dog soils the house, this further reinforces the dog's unfortunate preference for an indoor, carpeted toilet. Do not let an unhousetrained dog have full run of the house.

When you are away from home, or cannot pay full attention, confine the dog to an area where elimination is appropriate, such as an outdoor run or, better still, a small, comfortable indoor kennel with access to an outdoor run. When confined in this manner, most dogs will naturally housetrain themselves.

73

eliminating, it is only necessary to cover that part of the floor with newspaper. The smaller papered area may then be moved (only a little each day) towards the door to the outside. Thus the dog will develop the tendency to go to the door when she needs to relieve herself.

Never confine an unhousetrained dog to a crate for long periods. Doing so would force the dog to soil the crate and ruin its usefulness as an aid for housetraining (see the following discussion).

Teaching Where

In order to teach your dog where you would like her to do her business, you have to be there to direct the proceedings—an obvious, yet often neglected, fact of life. In order to be there to teach the dog where to go, you need to know *when* she needs to go. Indeed, the success of housetraining depends on the owner's ability to predict these times. Certainly, a regular feeding schedule will facilitate prediction somewhat, but there is nothing like "loading the deck" and influencing the timing of the outcome yourself!

Whenever you are at home, make sure the dog is under constant

Your Westie will never soil her close confinement area, which is why it is a good idea to have a crate handy when house-training.

If that's not possible, confine the dog to an area, such as a utility room, kitchen, basement or garage, where elimination may not be desired in the long run but as an interim measure it is certainly preferable to doing it all around the house. Use newspaper to cover the floor of the dog's day room. The newspaper may be used to soak up the urine and to wrap up and dispose of the feces. Once your dog develops a preferred spot for supervision and/or confined to a small area. If already well trained, simply instruct the dog to lie down in her bed or basket. Alternatively, confine the dog to a crate (doggy den) or tie-down (a short, 18-inch lead that can be clipped to an eye hook in the baseboard near her bed). Short-term close confinement strongly inhibits urination and defecation, since the dog does not want to soil her sleeping area. Thus, when you release the puppydog each hour, she will definitely need to urinate immediately and defecate every third or fourth hour. Keep the dog confined to her den and take her to her intended toilet area each hour, on the hour. When taking your dog outside, instruct her to sit quietly before opening the door—she will soon learn to sit by the door when she needs to go out!

Teaching Why

Being able to predict when the dog needs to go enables the owner to be on the spot to praise and reward the dog. Each hour, hurry the dog to the intended toilet area in the yard, issue the appropriate instruction ("Go pee!" or "Go poop!"), then give the dog three to four minutes to produce. Praise and offer a couple of training treats when successful. The treats are important because many people fail to praise their dogs with feeling . . . and housetraining is hardly the time for understatement. So either loosen up and enthusiastically praise that dog: "Wuzzzer-wuzzer-wuzzer, hoooser good wuffer den? Hoooo went pee for Daddy?" Or say "Good dog!" as best you can and offer the treats for effect.

Following elimination is an ideal time for a spot of play-training in the yard or house. Also, an empty dog may be allowed greater freedom around the house for the next half hour or so, just as long as you keep an eye out to make sure she does not get into other kinds of mischief. If you are preoccupied and cannot pay full attention, confine the dog to her doggy den once more to enjoy a peaceful snooze or to play with her many chew toys.

If your dog does not eliminate within the allotted time outside—no biggie! Back to her doggy den, and then try again after another hour.

As I own large dogs, I always feel more relaxed walking an empty dog, knowing that I will not need to finish our stroll weighted down with bags of feces!

Beware of falling into the trap of walking the dog to get her to eliminate. The good ol' dog walk is such an enormous highlight in the dog's life that it represents the single biggest potential reward in domestic dogdom. However, when in a hurry, or during inclement weather, many owners abruptly terminate the walk the moment the dog has done her business. This, in effect, severely punishes the dog for doing the right thing, in the right place at the right time. Consequently, many dogs become strongly inhibited from eliminating outdoors because they know it will signal an abrupt end to an otherwise thoroughly enjoyable walk.

Instead, instruct the dog to relieve herself in the yard prior to going for a walk. If you follow the above instructions, most dogs soon learn to eliminate on cue. As soon as the dog eliminates, praise (and offer a treat or two)—"Good dog! Let's go walkies!" Use the walk as a reward for eliminating in the yard. If the dog does not go, put her back in her doggy den and think about a walk later on. You will find with a "No feces—no walk" policy, your dog will become one of the fastest defecators in the business.

If you do not have a backyard, instruct the dog to eliminate right outside your front door prior to the walk. Not only will this facilitate

This Westie has an array of fun toys to choose from for when she is feeling bored or lonely or is in the mood to chew something to shreds.

clean up and disposal of the feces in your own trash can but, also, the walk may again be used as a colossal reward.

CHEWING AND BARKING

Short-term close confinement also teaches the dog that occasional quiet moments are a reality of domestic living. Your puppydog is extremely impressionable during her first few weeks at home. Regular confinement at this time soon exerts a calming influence over the dog's personality.

When confining the dog, make sure she always has an impressive array of suitable chew toys. Kongs and sterilized longbones (both readily available from pet stores) make the best chew toys, since they are hollow and may be stuffed with treats to heighten the dog's interest. For example, by stuffing the little hole at the top of a Kong with a small piece of freeze-dried liver, the dog will not want to leave it alone.

Remember, treats do not have to be junk food and they certainly should not represent extra calories. Rather, treats should be part of each dog's regular daily diet. I regularly

TOYS THAT EARN THEIR KEEP

To entertain even the most distracted of dogs, while you're home or away, have a selection of the following toys on hand: hollow chew toys (like Kongs, sterilized hollow longbones and cubes or balls that can be stuffed with kibble). Smear peanut butter or honey on the inside of the hollow toy or bone, stuff the bone with kibble and your dog will think of nothing else but working the object to get at the food. Great to take your dog's mind off the fact that you've left the house.

stuff my dogs' many Kongs with different shaped biscuits and kibble. The kibble seems to fall out fairly easily, as do the oval-shaped biscuits, thus rewarding the dog instantaneously for checking out the chew toys. The bone-shaped biscuits fall out after a while, rewarding the dog for worrying at the chew toy. But the triangular biscuits never come out. They remain inside the Kong as lures, maintaining the dog's fascination with her chew toy. To further focus the dog's interest, I always make sure to flavor the triangular biscuits by rubbing them with a little cheese or freeze-dried liver.

If stuffed chew toys are reserved especially for times the dog is confined, the puppydog will soon learn to enjoy quiet moments in her doggy den and she will quickly develop a chew-toy habit—a good habit! This is a simple autoshaping process; all the owner has to do is set up the situation and the dog all but trains herself—easy and effective. Even when the dog is given run of the house, her first inclination will be to indulge her rewarding chew-toy habit rather than destroy less-attractive household articles. Similarly, a chew-toy chewer will be less inclined to scratch and chew herself excessively. Also, if the dog busies herself as a recreational chewer, she will be less inclined to

It isn't hard to train your Westie, since all she wants to do is please you.

develop into a recreational barker or digger when left at home alone.

Stuff a number of chew toys whenever the dog is left confined and remove the extra-special-tasting treats when you return. Your dog will now amuse herself with her chew toys before falling asleep and then resume playing with her chew toys when she expects you to return.

COME AND SIT

Most puppies will happily approach virtually anyone, whether called or not; that is, until they collide with adolescence and develop other more important doggy interests, such as sniffing a multiplicity of exquisite odors on the grass. Your mission, Mr./Ms. Owner, is to teach and reward the pup for coming reliably, willingly and happily when called— and you have just three months to get it done. Unless adequately reinforced, your puppy's tendency to approach people will self-destruct by adolescence.

Call your dog ("Fido, come!"), open your arms (and maybe squat down) as a welcoming signal, waggle a treat or toy as a lure and reward the puppydog when she comes running. Do not wait to praise the dog until she reaches you—she may come 95 percent of the way and then run off after some distraction. Instead, praise the dog's first step towards you and continue praising enthusiastically for every step she takes in your direction.

When the rapidly approaching puppy dog is three lengths away from impact, instruct her to sit ("Fido, sit!") and hold the lure in front of you in an outstretched hand to prevent her from hitting you mid-chest and knocking you flat on your back! As Fido decelerates to nose the lure, move the treat upwards and backwards just over her muzzle with an upwards motion of your extended arm (palm-upwards). As the dog looks up to follow the lure, she will sit down (if she jumps up, you are holding the lure too high). Praise the dog for sitting. Move backwards and call her again. Repeat this many times over, always praising when Fido comes and sits; on occasion, reward her.

For the first couple of trials, use a training treat both as a lure to entice the dog to come and sit and as a reward for doing so. Thereafter, try to use different items as lures and rewards. For example, lure the dog with a Kong or Frisbee but reward her with a food treat. Or lure the dog with a food treat but pat her and throw a tennis ball as a reward. After just a few repetitions, dispense with the lures and rewards; the dog will begin to respond willingly to your verbal requests and hand signals just for the prospect of praise from your heart and affection from your hands.

Instruct every family member, friend and visitor how to get the dog to come and sit. Invite people over for a series of pooch parties; do not keep the pup a secret—let other people enjoy this puppy, and let the pup enjoy other people. Puppydog parties are not only fun, they easily attract a lot of people to help you train your dog. Unless you teach your dog how to meet people, that is, to sit for greetings, no doubt the dog will resort to jumping up. Then you and the visitors will get annoyed, and the dog will be punished. This is not fair. Send out those invitations for puppy parties and teach your dog to be mannerly and socially acceptable.

Even though your dog quickly masters obedient recalls in the house, her reliability may falter when playing in the backyard or local park. Ironically, it is the owner who has unintentionally trained the dog not to respond in these instances. By allowing the dog to play and run around and otherwise have a good time, but then to call the dog to put her on leash to take her home, the dog quickly learns playing is fun but training is a drag. Thus, playing in the park becomes a severe distraction, which works against training. Bad news!

Instead, whether playing with the dog off leash or on leash, request her to come at frequent intervals— say, every minute or so. On most occasions, praise and pet the dog for a few seconds while she is sitting, then tell her to go play again. For especially fast recalls, offer a couple of training treats and take the time to praise and pet the dog enthusiastically before releasing her. The dog will learn that coming when called is not necessarily the end of the play session, and neither is it the end of the world; rather, it signals an enjoyable, quality time-out with the owner before resuming play once more. In fact, playing in the park now becomes a very effective life-reward, which works to facilitate training by reinforcing each obedient and timely recall. Good news!

SIT, DOWN, STAND AND ROLLOVER

Teaching the dog a variety of body positions is easy for owner and dog, impressive for spectators and extremely useful for all. Using lure-reward techniques, it is possible to train several positions at once to verbal commands or hand signals (which impress the socks off onlookers).

Sit and down—the two control commands—prevent or resolve nearly a hundred behavior problems. For example, if the dog happily and obediently sits or lies down when requested, she cannot jump on visitors, dash out the front door, run around and chase her tail, pester other dogs, harass cats or annoy family, friends or strangers. Additionally, "Sit" or "Down" are the best emergency commands for off-leash control.

It is easier to teach and maintain a reliable sit than maintain a reliable recall. Sit is the purest and simplest of commands—either the dog is sitting or she is not. If there is any change of circumstances or potential danger in the park, for example, simply instruct the dog to sit. If she sits, you have a number of options:

Allow the dog to resume playing when she is safe, walk up and put the dog on leash or call the dog. The dog will be much more likely to come when called if she has already acknowledged her compliance by sitting. If the dog does not sit in the park—train her to!

Stand and rollover-stay are the two positions for examining the dog. Your veterinarian will love you to distraction if you take a little time to teach the dog to stand still and roll over and play possum. Also, your vet bills will be smaller because it will take the veterinarian less time to examine your dog. The rollover-stay is an especially useful command and is really just a variation of the down-stay: Whereas the dog lies prone in the traditional down, she lies supine in the rollover-stay.

As with teaching come and sit, the training techniques to teach the dog to assume all other body positions on cue are user-friendly and dog-friendly. Simply give the appropriate request, lure the dog into the desired body position using a training treat or toy and then praise (and maybe reward) the dog as soon as she complies. Try not to touch the dog to get her to respond. If you teach the dog by guiding her into

This woman holds out her arm and raises her palm to demonstrate the down command.

81

position, the dog will quickly learn that rump-pressure means sit, for example, but as yet you still have no control over your dog if she is just 6 feet away. It will still be necessary to teach the dog to sit on request. So do not make training a time-consuming two-step process; instead, teach the dog to sit to a verbal request or hand signal from the outset. Once the dog sits willingly when requested, by all means use your hands to pet the dog when she does so.

To teach down when the dog is already sitting, say "Fido, down!," hold the lure in one hand (palm down) and lower that hand to the floor between the dog's forepaws. As the dog lowers her head to follow the lure, slowly move the lure away from the dog just a fraction (in front of her paws). The dog will lie down as she stretches her nose forward to follow the lure. Praise the dog when she does so. If the dog stands up, you pulled the lure away too far and too quickly.

When teaching the dog to lie down from the standing position, say "Down" and lower the lure to the floor as before. Once the dog has lowered her forequarters and assumed a play bow, gently and slowly move the lure towards the dog between her forelegs. Praise the dog as soon as her rear end plops down.

After just a couple of trials it will be possible to alternate sits and downs and have the dog energetically perform doggy push-ups. Praise the dog a lot, and after half a dozen or so push-ups reward the dog with a training treat or toy. You will notice the more energetically you move your arm—upwards (palm up) to get the dog to sit, and downwards (palm down) to get the dog to lie down—the more energetically the dog responds to your requests. Now try training the dog in silence and you will notice she has also learned

to respond to hand signals. Yeah! Not too shabby for the first session.

To teach stand from the sitting position, say "Fido, stand," slowly move the lure half a dog-length away from the dog's nose, keeping it at nose level, and praise the dog as she stands to follow the lure. As soon as the dog stands, lower the lure to just beneath the dog's chin to entice her to look down; otherwise she will stand and then sit immediately. To prompt the dog to stand from the down position, move the lure half a dog-length upwards and away from the dog, holding the lure at standing nose height from the floor.

Teaching rollover is best started from the down position, with the dog lying on one side, or at least with both hind legs stretched out on the same side. Say "Fido, bang!" and move the lure backwards and alongside the dog's muzzle to her elbow (on the side of her outstretched hind legs). Once the dog looks to the side and backwards, very slowly move the lure upwards to the dog's shoulder and backbone. Tickling the dog in the goolies (groin area) often invokes a reflex-raising of the hind leg as an appeasement gesture, which facilitates the tendency to roll over. If you move the lure too quickly and the dog jumps into the standing position, have patience and start again. As soon as the dog rolls onto her back, keep the lure stationary and mesmerize the dog with a relaxing tummy rub.

To teach rollover-stay when the dog is standing or moving, say "Fido, bang!" and give the appropriate hand signal (with index finger pointed and thumb cocked in true Sam Spade fashion), then in one fluid movement lure her to first lie down and then rollover-stay as above.

Teaching the dog to stay in each of the above four positions becomes a piece of cake after first teaching

the dog not to worry at the toy or treat training lure. This is best accomplished by hand feeding dinner kibble. Hold a piece of kibble firmly in your hand and softly instruct "Off!" Ignore any licking and slobbering for however long the dog worries at the treat, but say "Take it!" and offer the kibble *the instant* the dog breaks contact with her muzzle. Repeat this a few times, and then up the ante and insist the dog remove her muzzle for one whole second before offering the kibble. Then progressively refine your criteria and have the dog not touch your hand (or treat) for longer and longer periods on each trial, such as for

83

Look at this girl go as she complies to her owner's signal to rollover!

two seconds, four seconds, then six, ten, fifteen, twenty, thirty seconds and so on.

The dog soon learns: (1) worrying at the treat never gets results, whereas (2) noncontact is often rewarded after a variable time lapse.

Teaching "Off!" has many useful applications in its own right. Additionally, instructing the dog not to touch a training lure often produces spontaneous and magical stays. Request the dog to stand-stay, for example, and not to touch the lure. At first set your sights on a short two-second stay before rewarding the dog. (Remember, every long journey begins with a single step.) However, on subsequent trials, gradually and progressively increase the length of stay required to receive a reward. In no time at all your dog will stand calmly for a minute or so.

RELEVANCY TRAINING

Once you have taught the dog what you expect her to do when requested to come, sit, lie down, stand, rollover and stay, the time is right to teach the dog why she should comply with

your wishes. The secret is to have many (many) extremely short training interludes (two to five seconds each) at numerous (numerous) times during the course of the dog's day. Especially work with the dog immediately before the dog's good times and during the dog's good times. For example, ask your dog to sit and/or lie down each time before opening doors, serving meals, offering treats and tummy rubs; ask the dog to perform a few controlled doggy push-ups before letting her off leash or throwing a tennis ball; and perhaps request the dog to sit-down-sit-stand-down-stand-rollover before inviting her to cuddle on the couch.

Similarly, request the dog to sit many times during play or on walks, and in no time at all the dog will be only too pleased to follow your instructions because she has learned that a compliant response heralds all sorts of goodies. Basically all you are trying to teach the dog is how to say please: "Please throw the tennis ball. Please may I snuggle on the couch."

Remember, it is important to keep training interludes short and to have many short sessions each and every day.

WALK BY YOUR SIDE

Many people attempt to teach a dog to heel by putting her on a leash and physically correcting the dog when she makes mistakes. There are a number of things seriously wrong with this approach, the first being that most people do not want precision heeling; rather, they simply want the dog to follow or walk by their side. Second, when physically restrained during "training," even though the dog may grudgingly mope by your side when "handcuffed" on leash, let's see what happens when she is off leash. History! The dog is in the next county because she never enjoyed walking with you on leash and you have no control over her off leash. So let's just teach the dog off leash from the outset to want to walk with us. Third, if the dog has not been trained to heel, it is a trifle hasty to think about punishing the poor dog for making mistakes and breaking heeling rules she didn't even know existed. This is simply not fair! Surely, if the dog had been adequately taught how to heel, she would seldom make mistakes and hence there would be no need to

You will want to show off your beautiful well-trained Westie.

correct the dog. Remember, each mistake and each correction (punishment) advertise the trainer's inadequacy, not the dog's. The dog is not stubborn, she is not stupid and she is not bad. Even if she were, she would still require training, so let's train her properly.

Let's teach the dog to enjoy following us and to want to walk by our side off leash. Then it will be easier to teach high-precision off-leash heeling patterns if desired. Before going on outdoor walks, it is necessary to teach the dog not to pull. Then it becomes easy to teach on-leash walking and heeling

85

This owner has trained her dog to walk calmly and confidently by her side.

because the dog already wants to walk with you, she is familiar with the desired walking and heeling positions and she knows not to pull.

FOLLOWING

Start by training your dog to follow you. Many puppies will follow if you simply walk away from them and maybe click your fingers or chuckle. Adult dogs may require additional enticement to stimulate them to follow, such as a training lure or, at the very least, a lively trainer. To teach the dog to follow: (1) keep walking and (2) walk away from the dog. If the dog attempts to lead or lag,

change pace; slow down if the dog forges too far ahead, but speed up if she lags too far behind. Say "Steady!" or "Easy!" each time before you slow down and "Quickly!" or "Hustle!" each time before you speed up, and the dog will learn to change pace on cue. If the dog lags or leads too far, or if she wanders right or left, simply walk quickly in the opposite direction and maybe even run away from the dog and hide.

Remember, following has a lot to do with attitude—your attitude! Most probably your dog will not want to follow Mr. Grumpy Troll with the personality of wilted lettuce. Lighten up—walk with a jaunty step, whistle a happy tune, sing, skip and tell jokes to your dog and she will be right there by your side.

NO PULLING ON LEASH

You can start teaching your dog not to pull on leash anywhere—in front of the television or outdoors—but regardless of location, you must not take a single step with tension in the leash. For a reason known only to dogs, even just a couple of paces of pulling on leash is intrinsically motivating and diabolically rewarding.

Instead, attach the leash to the dog's collar, grasp the other end firmly with both hands held close to your chest, and stand still—do not budge an inch. Have somebody watch you with a stopwatch to time your progress, or else you will never believe this will work and so you will not even try the exercise, and your shoulder and the dog's neck will be traumatized for years to come.

Stand still and wait for the dog to stop pulling, and to sit and/or lie down. All dogs stop pulling and sit eventually. Most take only a couple of minutes; the all-time record is 22 $\frac{1}{2}$ minutes. Time how long it takes. Gently praise the dog when she stops pulling, and as soon as she sits, enthusiastically praise the dog and take just one step forwards, then immediately stand still. This single step usually demonstrates the ballistic reinforcing nature of pulling on leash; most dogs explode to the end of the leash, so be prepared for the strain. Stand firm and wait for the dog to sit again. Repeat this half a dozen times and you will probably notice a progressive reduction in the force of the dog's one-step explosions and a radical reduction in the time it takes for the dog to sit each time.

As the dog learns "Sit we go" and "Pull we stop," she will begin to walk forward calmly with each single step and automatically sit when you stop. Now try two steps before you stop. Wooooooo! Scary! When the dog has mastered two steps at a time, try for three. After each success, progressively increase the number of steps in the sequence: try four steps and then six, eight, ten and twenty steps before stopping. Congratulations! You are now walking the dog on leash.

This dog walks with his owner at heel.

CHAPTER NINE

Resources

BOOKS

About West Highland White Terriers

Faherty, Ruth. *Westies from Head to Toe.* Loveland, CO: Alpine Publications, 1989.

Gentry, Daphne S. *The New West Highland White Terrier.* New York: Howell Book House, 1998.

Martin, Dawn. *A New Owner's Guide to West Highland White Terriers.* Neptune, NJ: TFH, 1996.

Tattersol, Derek. *Westies Today.* New York: Howell Book House, 1992.

About Health Care

American Kennel Club. *American Kennel Club Dog Care and Training.* New York: Howell Book House, 1991.

Carlson, Delbert, DVM, and James Giffen, MD. *Dog Owner's Home Veterinary Handbook.* New York: Howell Book House, 1992.

DeBitetto, James, DVM, and Sarah Hodgson. *You & Your Puppy.* New York: Howell Book House, 1995.

Lane, Marion. *The Humane Society of the United States Complete Guide to Dog Care.* New York: Little, Brown & Co., 1998.

McGinnis, Terri. *The Well Dog Book.* New York: Random House, 1991.

Schwartz, Stephanie, DVM. *First Aid for Dogs: An Owner's Guide to a Happy Healthy Pet.* New York: Howell Book House, 1998.

Volhard, Wendy and Kerry L. Brown. *The Holistic Guide for a Healthy Dog.* New York: Howell Book House, 1995.

About Training

Ammen, Amy. *Training in No Time.* New York: Howell Book House, 1995.

Benjamin, Carol Lea. *Mother Knows Best.* New York: Howell Book House, 1985.

Bohnenkamp, Gwen. *Manners for the Modern Dog.* San Francisco: Perfect Paws, 1990.

Dunbar, Ian, Ph.D., MRCVS. *Dr. Dunbar's Good Little Book.* James & Kenneth Publishers, 2140 Shattuck Ave. #2406, Berkeley, CA 94704. (510) 658-8588. Order from Publisher.

Evans, Job Michael. *People, Pooches and Problems.* New York: Howell Book House, 1991.

Palika, Liz. *All Dogs Need Some Training.* New York: Howell Book House, 1997.

Volhard, Jack and Melissa Bartlett. *What All Good Dogs Should Know: The Sensible Way to Train.* New York: Howell Book House, 1991.

MAGAZINES

The AKC GAZETTE, The Official Journal for the Sport of Purebred Dogs
American Kennel Club
260 Madison Ave.
New York, NY 10016
www.akc.org

Dog Fancy
Fancy Publications
3 Burroughs
Irvine, CA 92618
(714) 855-8822
http://dogfancy.com

Dog & Kennel
7-L Dundas Circle
Greensboro, NC 27407
(336) 292-4047
www.dogandkennel.com

Dog World
Maclean Hunter Publishing Corp.
500 N. Dearborn, Ste. 1100
Chicago, IL 60610
(312) 396-0600
www.dogworldmag.com

PetLife: Your Companion Animal Magazine
Magnolia Media Group
1400 Two Tandy Center
Fort Worth, TX 76102
(800) 767-9377
www.petlifeweb.com

MORE INFORMATION ABOUT WEST HIGHLAND WHITE TERRIERS

National Breed Club

WEST HIGHLAND WHITE TERRIER CLUB OF AMERICA

Corresponding Secretary:
  Berna Gaul
  4347 Camelot Circle
  Naperville, IL 60564
  (F): (630) 416-0776

Breeder Contact:
  Westie Information
  1085 Ripley Drive
  Charleston, SC 29412

Breed Rescue:
  Nancy Guilfoil
  (P): (314) 991-8819
  (F): (314) 991-7710

The Club can send you information on all aspects of the breed, including the names and addresses of breed clubs in your area, as well as obedience clubs. Inquire about membership.

The American Kennel Club

The American Kennel Club (AKC), devoted to the advancement of purebred dogs, is the oldest and largest registry organization in this country. Every breed recognized by the AKC has a national (parent) club. National clubs are a great source of information on your breed. The affiliated clubs hold AKC events and use AKC rules to hold performance events, dog shows, educational programs, health clinics and training classes. The AKC staff is divided between offices in New York City and Raleigh, North Carolina. The AKC has an excellent web site that provides information on the organization and all AKC-recognized breeds. The address is www.akc.org.

For registration and performance events information, or for customer service, contact:

THE AMERICAN KENNEL CLUB
5580 Centerview Dr., Suite 200
Raleigh, NC 27606
(919) 233-9767

The AKC's executive offices and the AKC Library (open to the public) are at this address:

THE AMERICAN KENNEL CLUB
260 Madison Ave.
New York, New York 10016
(212) 696-8200 (general information)
(212) 696-8246 (AKC Library)
www.akc.org

UNITED KENNEL CLUB
100 E. Kilgore Rd.
Kalamazoo, MI 49001-5598
(616) 343-9020
www.ukcdogs.com

AMERICAN RARE BREED ASSOCIATION
9921 Frank Tippett Rd.
Cheltenham, MD 20623
(301) 868-5718 (voice or fax)
www.arba.org

CANADIAN KENNEL CLUB
89 Skyway Ave., Ste. 100
Etobicoke, Ontario
Canada M9W 6R4
(416) 675-5511
www.ckc.ca

ORTHOPEDIC FOUNDATION FOR ANIMALS (OFA)
2300 E. Nifong Blvd.
Columbia, MO 65201-3856
(314) 442-0418
www.offa.org/

Trainers

Animal Behavior & Training Associates (ABTA)
9018 Balboa Blvd., Ste. 591
Northridge, CA 91325
(800) 795-3294
www.Good-dawg.com

Association of Pet Dog Trainers
(APDT)
P.O. Box 385
Davis, CA 95617
(800) PET-DOGS
www.apdt.com

National Association of Dog Obedience
Instructors (NADOI)
729 Grapevine Highway, Ste. 369
Hurst, TX 76054-2085
www.kimberly.uidaho.edu/nadoi

Associations

Delta Society
P.O. Box 1080
Renton, WA 98507-1080
(Promotes the human/animal bond
through pet-assisted therapy and other
programs)
www.petsform.com/detta/dsf000.htm

Dog Writers Association of America
(DWAA)
Sally Cooper, Secretary
222 Woodchuck Lane
Harwinton, CT 06791
http://dwaa.org

National Association for Search and
Rescue (NASAR)
4500 Southgate Place, Ste. 100
Chantilly, VA 20157
(703) 222-6277
www.nasar.org

Therapy Dogs International
6 Hilltop Rd.
Mendham, NJ 07945

OTHER USEFUL RESOURCES—WEB SITES

General Information— Links to Additional Sites, On-Line Shopping

www.k9web.com – resources for the dog
world

www.netpet.com – pet related products,
software and services

www.apapets.com – The American Pet
Association

www.dogandcatbooks.com – book catalog

www.dogbooks.com – on-line bookshop

www.animal.discovery.com/ – cable
television channel on-line

Health

www.avma.org – American Veterinary
Medical Association (AVMA)

www.aplb.org – Association for Pet Loss
Bereavement (APLB)—contains an
index of national hot lines for on-line
and office counseling.

www.netfopets.com/asktheexperts.html –
veterinary questions answered on-line

Breed Information

http://rec.pets.dogs.breeds – newsgroup

www/cheta.net/connect/canine/breeds/ –
Canine Connections Breed
Information Index

91